Dietary Supplements

Other Books of Related Interest

Opposing Viewpoints Series

Doping

Medical Marijuana

Prescription Drug Abuse

At Issue Series

Club Drugs

Extending the Human Lifespan

Should the Government Regulate What People Eat?

Should Vaccinations Be Mandatory?

Current Controversies Series

Medical Ethics

Prescription Drugs

"Congress shall make no law . . . abridging the freedom of speech, or of the press."

First Amendment to the US Constitution

The basic foundation of our democracy is the First Amendment guarantee of freedom of expression. The Opposing Viewpoints Series is dedicated to the concept of this basic freedom and the idea that it is more important to practice it than to enshrine it.

OPPOSING VIEWPOINTS® SERIES

Dietary Supplements

Noah Berlatsky, Book Editor

GREENHAVEN PRESS

A part of Gale, Cengage Learning

GALE
CENGAGE Learning®

Farmington Hills, Mich • San Francisco • New York • Waterville, Maine
Meriden, Conn • Mason, Ohio • Chicago

Elizabeth Des Chenes, *Director, Content Strategy*
Cynthia Sanner, *Publisher*
Douglas Dentino, *Manager, New Product*

For more information, contact:
Greenhaven Press
27500 Drake Rd.
Farmington Hills, MI 48331-3535
Or you can visit our Internet site at gale.cengage.com

For product information and technology assistance, contact us at

Gale Customer Support, 1-800-877-4253
For permission to use material from this text or product, submit all requests online at www.cengage.com/permissions

Further permissions questions can be emailed to permissionrequest@cengage.com

Articles in Greenhaven Press anthologies are often edited for length to meet page requirements. In addition, original titles of these works are changed to clearly present the main thesis and to explicitly indicate the author's opinion. Every effort is made to ensure that Greenhaven Press accurately reflects the original intent of the authors. Every effort has been made to trace the owners of copyrighted material.

Cover image © Pixelbliss/Shutterstock.com.

LIBRARY OF CONGRESS CATALOGING-IN-PUBLICATION DATA

Dietary supplements / Noah Berlatsky, book editor.
    pages cm. -- (Opposing viewpoints)
    Includes bibliographical references and index.
    ISBN 978-0-7377-6316-4 (hardcover) -- ISBN 978-0-7377-6317-1 (pbk.)
    1. Dietary supplements--Juvenile literature. I. Berlatsky, Noah, editor of compilation.
    RM258.5.D542 2014
    615.1--dc23

                                      2013043017

Printed in the United States of America
1 2 3 4 5 6 7 18 17 16 15 14

Contents

Chapter 3: Are Weight-Loss Supplements and Athletic Supplements Beneficial?

Chapter 4: How Well Do Supplements Treat Different Medical Conditions?

Why Consider
Opposing Viewpoints?

> *"The only way in which a human being can make some approach to knowing the whole of a subject is by hearing what can be said about it by persons of every variety of opinion and studying all modes in which it can be looked at by every character of mind. No wise man ever acquired his wisdom in any mode but this."*
>
> *John Stuart Mill*

In our media-intensive culture it is not difficult to find differing opinions. Thousands of newspapers and magazines and dozens of radio and television talk shows resound with differing points of view. The difficulty lies in deciding which opinion to agree with and which "experts" seem the most credible. The more inundated we become with differing opinions and claims, the more essential it is to hone critical reading and thinking skills to evaluate these ideas. Opposing Viewpoints books address this problem directly by presenting stimulating debates that can be used to enhance and teach these skills. The varied opinions contained in each book examine many different aspects of a single issue. While examining these conveniently edited opposing views, readers can develop critical thinking skills such as the ability to compare and contrast authors' credibility, facts, argumentation styles, use of persuasive techniques, and other stylistic tools. In short, the Opposing Viewpoints Series is an ideal way to attain the higher-level thinking and reading skills so essential in a culture of diverse and contradictory opinions.

In addition to providing a tool for critical thinking, Opposing Viewpoints books challenge readers to question their own strongly held opinions and assumptions. Most people form their opinions on the basis of upbringing, peer pressure, and personal, cultural, or professional bias. By reading carefully balanced opposing views, readers must directly confront new ideas as well as the opinions of those with whom they disagree. This is not to argue simplistically that everyone who reads opposing views will—or should—change his or her opinion. Instead, the series enhances readers' understanding of their own views by encouraging confrontation with opposing ideas. Careful examination of others' views can lead to the readers' understanding of the logical inconsistencies in their own opinions, perspective on why they hold an opinion, and the consideration of the possibility that their opinion requires further evaluation.

Evaluating Other Opinions

To ensure that this type of examination occurs, Opposing Viewpoints books present all types of opinions. Prominent spokespeople on different sides of each issue as well as well-known professionals from many disciplines challenge the reader. An additional goal of the series is to provide a forum for other, less known, or even unpopular viewpoints. The opinion of an ordinary person who has had to make the decision to cut off life support from a terminally ill relative, for example, may be just as valuable and provide just as much insight as a medical ethicist's professional opinion. The editors have two additional purposes in including these less known views. One, the editors encourage readers to respect others' opinions—even when not enhanced by professional credibility. It is only by reading or listening to and objectively evaluating others' ideas that one can determine whether they are worthy of consideration. Two, the inclusion of such viewpoints encourages the important critical thinking skill of objectively evaluating an author's credentials and bias. This evaluation will illuminate an author's reasons for taking a particular stance on an issue and will aid in readers' evaluation of the author's ideas.

It is our hope that these books will give readers a deeper understanding of the issues debated and an appreciation of the complexity of even seemingly simple issues when good and honest people disagree. This awareness is particularly important in a democratic society such as ours in which people enter into public debate to determine the common good. Those with whom one disagrees should not be regarded as enemies but rather as people whose views deserve careful examination and may shed light on one's own.

Thomas Jefferson once said that "difference of opinion leads to inquiry, and inquiry to truth." Jefferson, a broadly educated man, argued that "if a nation expects to be ignorant and free . . . it expects what never was and never will be." As individuals and as a nation, it is imperative that we consider the opinions of others and examine them with skill and discernment. The Opposing Viewpoints Series is intended to help readers achieve this goal.

David L. Bender and Bruno Leone,
Founders

Introduction

> *"Soon after our passing straits Le Maire, the scurvy began to make its appearance amongst us: and our long continuance at sea, the fatigue we underwent, and the various disappointments we met with, had occasioned its spreading to such a degree, that at the latter end of April, there were but few on board who were not in some degree afflicted with it."*
>
> —*Richard Walter,*
> *surgeon under*
> *Commodore George Anson, 1748*

Disease raged throughout the six ships of Commodore George Anson's command. He had sailed from Britain into the Pacific in the 1740s on a mission to raid Spanish ships. But then, tragedy struck. The disease was terrible; men's skin turned ink black; their limbs froze; they could not breathe; their teeth fell out, and gum tissue poked out of their mouths, immediately rotting and giving their breath a deadly smell. They also suffered acute psychological distress and lost control of their emotions and senses. According to a February 17, 2011, article by Jonathan Lamb on the British Broadcasting Corporation (BBC) website, "The sound of a gunshot was enough to kill a man" suffering from the disease, "while the smell of blossoms from the shore could cause him to cry out in agony."

The disease in question was not really a disease. It was not caused by a parasite or microbial infection but by a nutritional deficiency. Anson's sailors were suffering from scurvy, resulting from the lack of vitamin C, which plays an important role in the body's production of collagen, or connective tissue. Without it, the cellular structure of the body breaks down. Usually this does not happen, since Vitamin C is plentiful in fruits and vegetables. If you have a varied diet, in most cases you will have enough vitamin C in your body to prevent scurvy. However, on board ship, sailors' diets were restricted, often including little fruit or other fresh foods. The resulting scurvy was inevitably fatal if not treated.

But how do you treat scurvy? To find the answer, James Lind conducted an experiment on board the British ship HMS *Salisbury* in 1747. He gave some members of the crew various treatments in addition to their regular rations. Among the treatments he tested were cider, acid, seawater, and lemons. To his excitement, he found that the sailors who received the lemons recovered quickly from scurvy. All the others simply got sicker and sicker.

It would take a while for Lind's findings to be accepted, Finally, in 1790 the British navy officially began providing lemons to its sailors, allowing sailors to stay much longer at sea. As a result, long-term naval blockades became possible. Thus, the cure for scurvy played an important strategic role in the Napoleonic Wars.

Though lemons are, of course, a food, they were essentially being used by the navy as a dietary supplement, to provide additional nutrients or benefits to sailors. However, *why* the lemons worked was not well understood. The idea that the body needed certain nutrients to function was not developed until the 1840s. Lind himself did not realize that the lemons were adding vital vitamin C missing from the sailors' diets.

The results of this lack of understanding were tragic. Because citrus is acidic, for example, some people believed that any acid could be used as a dietary supplement instead of citrus fruit. Thus, instead of lemons, the Royal Navy sometimes used limes, which had less vitamin C and were less effective. Even worse, they would substitute lime juice. The juice had often been exposed to the air for long periods and had lost its vitamin C. Inevitably, scurvy began to make a comeback among sailors. The fact that lemon juice was a cure had to be rediscovered early in the 1900s.

The history of scurvy, then, is in part a history of the potential effectiveness and potential failures of dietary supplements. On the one hand, using lemons as a supplement to rations provided an instant, almost miraculous cure for a terrible, deadly, formerly untreatable condition. On the other hand, other supplements were not scientifically tested and failed to provide the same benefits. In fact, substances like lime juice were worse than nothing at all, because they confused the issue. People believed that they had a cure when they did not, and scientific knowledge about the treatment of scurvy was essentially lost for decades.

Scurvy is now quite rare in the West, and vitamin C is a popular dietary supplement in its own right. The viewpoints in this book debate the value of vitamin C supplements, and many other supplements, in four chapters, titled How Should Dietary Supplements Be Regulated?, Are Vitamin and Mineral Supplements Beneficial?, Are Weight-Loss Supplements and Athletic Supplements Beneficial?, and How Well Do Supplements Treat Different Medical Conditions? The authors debate the ways in which dietary supplements may be effective and useful, like lemons for scurvy, and ways in which, like lime juice, they may not be so useful.

How Should Dietary Supplements Be Regulated?

Chapter Preface

How should dietary supplements be regulated? Different countries have come up with different answers. In the United States, the Dietary Supplement Health and Education Act of 1994 exempts dietary supplements from Food and Drug Administration (FDA) regulations for over-the-counter and prescription drugs. This means that manufacturers do not need to receive FDA approval before putting a supplement on the market. Supplements are supposed to be safe, and they are not supposed to make misleading claims. But safety and effectiveness are evaluated only after the products go on the market. Many dietary supplements in the United States, therefore, are not scientifically proven to be effective.

In Canada, the system is different. Health Canada (the Canadian equivalent of the FDA) established the National Health Products Directorate (NHPD) in 2004. The NHPD licenses dietary supplements before they are allowed on the market. Products that cannot be shown to be effective scientifically, or that are unsafe, are denied licenses. Since 2004, a full 48 percent of supplements submitted to the NHPD have been rejected or withdrawn because they fail to meet scientific and/or safety standards.

It might be argued that the Canadian approach is more rigorous than the US one; however, the NHPD has its problems. There is a huge backlog of product applications, and the NHPD has had trouble evaluating supplements in a timely manner. Because of this, enforcement is haphazard. The NHPD tries to focus on high-risk supplements, such as those for pregnant women. Thus, while it is technically illegal to market a supplement in Canada without a license, in practice many supplements are sold without a license and without interference by the government.

Another problem with the Canadian system is that the standards for evaluating supplements can be haphazard. Scientific trials are not necessary; in many cases, companies can make health claims based on "anecdotal efficacy of use and efficiency," according to Scott Gavura in an August 5, 2010, post at the blog *Science-Based Medicine*. The Canadian government, in other words, licenses substances with no scientific data, on the basis of testimonials or tradition. Arguably, this gives the force of government approval to nonscientific claims. This may be more misleading than the American approach, where the government allows supplements to be sold without scientific evidence of effectiveness, but at least does not officially approve them.

The viewpoints in this chapter debate issues around government regulation of dietary supplements in both the United States and Europe.

| "Even when the [FDA] identifies an un-
safe product, it lacks authority to mandate its removal from the market."

Natural Does Not Mean Safe

Geoffrey Kabat

Geoffrey Kabat is a cancer epidemiologist at the Albert Einstein College of Medicine in New York City and the author of Hyping Health Risks: Environmental Hazards in Daily Life and the Science of Epidemiology. *In the following viewpoint, he argues that dietary and herbal supplements need stricter oversight from the Food and Drug Administration (FDA). He contends that dietary supplements are widely used and often have adverse effects and that the FDA needs the ability to quickly restrict supplements that cause adverse effects. Currently, he argues, consumers are exposed to dangerous substances and the FDA has little ability to act.*

As you read, consider the following questions:

1. What is DSHEA, and how did it affect the number of dietary supplements on the market between 1994 and 2008, according to Kabat?

2. What major deficiencies does the author say that Donald Marcus and Arthur Grollman point out regarding the regulation of dietary supplements?

3. How was Aristolochia's toxicity discovered, according to Kabat?

This past October [2012], the office of the inspector general of the Department of Health and Human Services issued two reports underscoring the need for improved oversight of the marketing of dietary supplements and improved surveillance of their effects. The reports add to a mounting body of evidence documenting a serious public-health problem.

More Supplements, More Ill Effects

Use of dietary and herbal supplements has grown dramatically in recent years in the United States. In 2007, according to the National Center for Complementary and Alternative Medicine, $14.8 billion was spent on nonvitamin, nonmineral, natural products, such as fish oil, glucosamine, and Echinacea—equivalent to approximately one-third of total out-of-pocket spending on prescription drugs. Of that total, $4.4 billion was spent on herbal supplements. Data from the National Health and Nutrition Survey for 2003 to 2006 indicate that one-half of American adults use dietary supplements and 20 percent use a supplement with at least one botanical ingredient.

Many people think that because herbs are natural, and because they are being marketed and sold legally, they must be safe and effective. Furthermore, surveys of the public indicate that most people believe these products are regulated by the U.S. Food and Drug Administration. In fact, both assumptions are mistaken.

In 1994, Congress passed the Dietary Supplement Health and Education Act, with heavy backing from the dietary supplements industry. By defining herbal supplements and botanicals as dietary supplements, DSHEA exempted them from the more rigorous standards used by the FDA in regulating food, drugs, and medical devices—essentially leaving it up to the industry to regulate itself. This single piece of legislation opened the floodgates to a rapid expansion in the sale of dietary supplements.

Between 1994 and 2008, the number of dietary supplement products on the market increased from 4,000 to 75,000. In the first 10 months of 2008, the FDA received nearly 600 reports of serious adverse events (including hospitalization, disability, and death) from these products and 350 reports of moderate or mild adverse events. However, the FDA believes that these reports are drastically underreported and estimates that the annual number of all adverse events is 50,000.

More Authority Needed

Two highly respected physician-scientists, Donald Marcus of Baylor College of Medicine and Arthur Grollman of Stony Brook University, have been drawing attention to the dangers of herbal supplements for more than a decade. In a recent article in the *Archives of Internal Medicine*, they noted, "Even when the agency [FDA] identifies an unsafe product, it lacks authority to mandate its removal from the market because it must meet the very high legal requirement to demonstrate a 'significant or unreasonable' risk. That is why it took FDA more than 10 years to remove from the market ephedra-containing herbal weight-loss products that had caused hundreds of deaths and thousands of adverse events."

Marcus and Grollman point to a number of major deficiencies in the regulation of herbal supplements: There is a lack of standardization to guard against adulteration and ensure a consistent level of the active ingredients. Herbal supplements can interact adversely with prescribed drugs. Herbal supplements do not need to be tested before marketing, as is

Ephedra and the FDA

On February 11, 2004, the Food and Drug Administration (FDA) issued a final ruling that banned the sale of ephedra-containing supplements in the United States. The effective date of the ban was April 12, 2004, giving supplement makers 2 months to pull their supplements containing ephedra or ephedrine alkaloids off the market. This action banning ephedra was the first time the FDA had taken a formal action to halt the sale of a dietary supplement ingredient since the passage of DSHEA in 1994. This final ruling was made after an extensive review of the reports of adverse events, a review of scientific literature on the pharmacology of ephedrine and ephedrine alkaloids, and peer-reviewed scientific literature on the effects of ephedrine alkaloids.

The ephedrine alkaloids, including, among others, ephedrine, pseudoephedrine, norephedrine, methylephedrine, norpseudoephedrine, and methylpseudoephedrine, are chemical stimulants that occur naturally in some botanicals (plants) but can also be synthetically derived. Ma huang, ephedra, Chinese ephedra, and epitonin are several names used for botanical ingredients that are sources of ephedrine alkaloids. The commercial common name used for these substances is "ephedra," but ephedrine alkaloids are the actual ingredient source in the dietary supplements. Over the last decade dietary supplements containing ephedrine alkaloids have been labeled and used primarily for weight loss, increased energy, or to enhance athletic performance.

Heather Hedrick Fink, Alan E. Mikesky and Liza A. Burgoon,
Practical Applications in Sports Nutrition, 3rd edition
Burlington, MA: Jones & Bartlett Learning, 2012, p. 266.

required for prescription and over-the-counter drugs. Producers of dietary supplements engage in deceptive marketing and do not adequately label products to inform consumers about their nature and regulation. Finally, there is no requirement to report all adverse effects promptly to the FDA.

This lack of safeguards creates a situation in which unwitting consumers are exposed to herbal products that in most cases have no proven effectiveness but often have serious toxicities. Though we tend to equate *natural* with *healthy*, plants have developed toxins to protect themselves against predators. The perception that herbal supplements and botanicals are inherently safe is belied by extensive evidence of the danger posed by such products, including kava, ephedra, comfrey, and aristolochic acid. However, intensive advertising by the dietary supplements industry exploits and reinforces the illusion that plant products are inherently beneficial and harmless. In addition, the field of complementary and alternative medicine, which came to prominence in the 1990s, has helped to give a veneer of legitimacy to the use of supplements, even though this discipline is held in disrepute by scientists like Marcus and Grollman.

Natural Does Not Equal Healthy

The most dramatic instance of the potential for harm from the unregulated use of botanicals occurred in Brussels, Belgium. Women attending a weight-loss clinic participated in a program that involved taking a combination of Chinese herbs. The program had been in operation for 15 years with no ill effects. However, in the early 1990s, the company that supplied the herbs substituted *Aristolochia* for another, benign, herb with a similar sounding name in Chinese. *Aristolochia* has been widely used in herbal medicine, but it contains aristolochic acid—a powerful kidney toxin and a carcinogen. As a result of including *Aristolochia* in the regimen (for a period of two years), 105 women attending the clinic developed rapidly progressing kidney failure and had to go on dialysis or have kidney transplants. Many of the women went on to develop cancer of the upper urinary tract. Cases of kidney failure due to the ingestion of herbal products containing aristolochic acid have also been reported in the United States, Europe, and Asia.

This dramatic case led the FDA to issue a warning regarding products containing aristolochic acid, and some countries banned these products, including the United Kingdom, the Netherlands, Germany, and Japan. However, in spite of these restrictions, products containing aristolochic acid are still available on the Internet. What is essential to realize is that the effects of *Aristolochia* were identified only thanks to the large cluster of cases of kidney failure occurring in young women who had attended the same spa. It is much more likely that isolated cases will go unnoticed, as happened with ephedra, and it could take years to identify a common cause.

People failed to recognize the nephrotoxic effects of *Aristolochia* in spite of its use in many cultures worldwide over thousands of years. In an interview, Grollman explained why: "The reason, of course, is quite simple. It's painless, and the damage happens much later, so you don't put together the fact that you took this medicine and four years later, you have kidney failure. It's been part of Ayurvedic, European, Chinese, and South American medicine for centuries. All of the great civilizations have used it. And not one reported its toxicity until the Belgians did 20 years ago. There are certain things that tradition can't tell you."

In the political campaign that just ended [in November 2012], we heard a lot about the evils of regulation. But regulation cannot be judged in the abstract, without reference to the pertinent facts in the real world or the lives of real people. The recent outbreak of fungal meningitis caused by contamination of a steroid produced by a compounding company in Massachusetts underscores the potential for lapses even in the case of products that do come under the purview of the FDA. All the more reason why dietary and herbal supplements ought to be subject to at least as rigorous safeguards as those that apply to prescription and over-the-counter medications.

> *"DSHEA provides FDA with appropriate regulatory authority while still allowing consumers to have the desired access to a wide variety of affordable, high quality, safe and beneficial dietary supplement products."*

Current FDA Regulations Keep the Dietary Supplement Industry Beneficial and Safe

Council for Responsible Nutrition

The Council for Responsible Nutrition (CRN) is the leading trade association representing dietary supplement manufacturers and ingredient suppliers. In the following viewpoint, the CRN argues that dietary supplements are closely regulated by the Food and Drug Administration (FDA) and Federal Trade Commission (FTC) under the Dietary Supplement Health and Education Act (DSHEA). The CRN contends that government regulations ensure that dietary supplements are safe and notes that current laws have been used to remove unsafe dietary supplements from the market.

As you read, consider the following questions:

1. According to the CRN, what do critics mean when they say that dietary supplements are unregulated?

2. What evidence does the CRN provide that premarket approval of substances is not a guarantee of safety?

3. What is a GMP, as described by the author?

Who is the dietary supplement industry?

In the U.S., the dietary supplement industry is a $32 billion[1] industry. Dietary supplement products include vitamins, minerals, botanicals, sports nutrition supplements, weight management products and specialty supplements. These products are intended to be used as supplements to, not substitutes for, a well-balanced diet and a healthy lifestyle. When used properly, they help promote overall good health and prevent disease. More than 150 million Americans take dietary supplements annually.

Regulation of Supplements

Is the dietary supplement industry regulated?

Yes. The dietary supplement industry is regulated by FDA [Food and Drug Administration] and the Federal Trade Commission (FTC), as well as by government agencies in each of the 50 states. The FDA has regulatory authority under the Federal Food, Drug and Cosmetic Act as amended in 1994 by the Dietary Supplement Health and Education Act (DSHEA) and in 2006 by the Dietary Supplement and Nonprescription Drug Consumer Protection Act.

Why do some people say the industry is unregulated?

When critics say dietary supplements are "unregulated," what they generally mean is that dietary supplements are not regu-

1. 2011 *Nutritional Business Journal*

Areas Regulated by the FDA for Selected Product Types

	Foods	Dietary supplements	Drugs	Biologics	Medical devices
Pre-market approval			✓	✓	✓
Pre-market notification	✓	✓			
Labeling	✓	✓	✓	✓	✓
Mandatory adverse event reporting		✓	✓	✓	✓
GMPs	✓	✓	✓	✓	✓
Facility registration	✓	✓	✓	✓	✓
Advertising*	FTC	FTC	FDA	FDA	FDA

*Food and Drug Administration (FDA) or Federal Trade Commission (FTC).

TAKEN FROM: Council for Responsible Nutrition, "Regulations at a Glance," www.crnusa.org.

lated like drugs. Dietary supplements have always been regulated as a category of food in this country, and DSHEA did not change that fact. Virtually all facets of dietary supplement manufacturing, labeling and marketing are covered by extensive regulations issued and enforced by FDA and FTC. If dietary supplements were regulated like drugs, there would likely be no dietary supplement industry and the products that did exist would cost what drugs cost.

Is it true that before DSHEA was passed in 1994, FDA had pre-market approval authority?

No. FDA never had pre-market approval over dietary supplements, and DSHEA did not change that fact. Under the law, dietary supplements marketed in the U.S. before passage of DSHEA are "grandfathered" and assumed to have a history of safe use. If a supplement manufacturer wants to introduce a new ingredient, it must provide FDA with 75 days' notice, along with safety information. If FDA has any concerns about the ingredient or submitted safety profile, the agency can request more information or deny the product's entry into the marketplace. Since the passage of DSHEA, FDA has turned down about half of the New Dietary Ingredient notifications filed.

Without pre-market approval, how do we know these products are safe?

Pre-market approval is not a guarantee of safety as witnessed by those drug products that have been approved by FDA, only to be later recalled due to safety concerns. Like food products, dietary supplements do not undergo pre-market approval, but that does not mean that companies don't do testing, or that products are unsafe. There are provisions under DSHEA that protect consumers from potentially unsafe products. But the overwhelming majority of dietary supplements are safely used by 150 million Americans annually.

What DSHEA Does

What did DSHEA do?

DSHEA specifically reaffirmed the status of dietary supplements as a category of food and created a specific definition for dietary supplements. Further, DSHEA provided FDA with additional enforcement authority, including the ability to remove from the market products the agency deems unsafe through: 1) an "imminent hazard" clause that permits FDA to immediately remove a product it considers to present an immediate safety concern and 2) a "significant or unreasonable risk" clause that allows removal of a product considered to pose an unacceptable risk of illness or injury.

Shouldn't companies have to abide by Good Manufacturing Practices (GMPs)?

Absolutely. It's the law. Responsible companies *do* abide by GMPs—and many observe procedures which go above and beyond what the current regulations require. In June 2007, GMPs specific to dietary supplements were released from FDA. The GMP rule provided a staggered three-year "phase in" compliance period for manufacturers. And for large companies—more than 500 employees—the compliance date was June 2008. Firms with less than 500 employees had to be compliant by June 2009, and for small manufacturers that employ less than 20 employees, the compliance date was June 2010. Responsible companies in the industry have fully supported the need for dietary supplements GMPs in order to create a level playing field for companies across the board and help increase consumer confidence in the quality and safety of these products.

Should serious adverse events associated with dietary supplements be reported to FDA?

Yes. CRN [the Council on Responsible Nutrition] and mainstream industry supported the Dietary Supplement and Nonprescription Drug Consumer Protection Act which passed the 109th Congress and was signed into law by President [George W.] Bush on December 22, 2006. The law requires manufacturers to notify the FDA of all *serious* adverse events associated with an over-the-counter drug or a dietary supplement that they receive. This law strengthens the regulatory structure for dietary supplements and builds greater consumer confidence in this category of FDA-regulated products—thus ensuring and protecting Americans' continued access to safe, beneficial dietary supplements. Consumers have a right to expect that if they report a serious adverse event to a dietary supplement manufacturer, FDA will know about it.

Is DSHEA a good law?

Yes. DSHEA provides an appropriate framework for regulating the dietary supplement industry—as long as it is enforced. In the past several years, FDA has actively engaged in more vigorous implementation of DSHEA and stronger enforcement actions—these efforts are encouraged and supported by the mainstream dietary supplement industry. Even top officials at FDA have stated they are not asking Congress to change the law, noting they have adequate authority to remove unsafe supplements from the market. DSHEA provides FDA with appropriate regulatory authority while still allowing consumers to have the desired access to a wide variety of affordable, high quality, safe and beneficial dietary supplement products.

"Some customers have suffered serious health problems linked to [supplement] companies' poor manufacturing practices."

Dietary Supplements: Manufacturing Troubles Widespread, FDA Inspections Show

Trine Tsouderos

Trine Tsouderos is a science and medical journalist at the Chicago Tribune. *In the following viewpoint, he reports on the discovery by the Food and Drug Administration (FDA) that many dietary supplement companies violate manufacturing rules. The FDA discovered manufacturing plants infested with rodents and soiled by rodent feces. In other instances, Tsouderos says, the FDA found that products did not contain the ingredients on the label in the amounts specified. In some cases, these manufacturing failures resulted in poisonings or health problems for users. Tsouderos concludes that the dietary supplement industry needs to do better in following manufacturing guidelines and creating safe products.*

As you read, consider the following questions:

1. What percentage of dietary supplement companies inspected by the FDA have received warning letters, according to Tsouderos?

2. What was Quality Formulation Laboratories convicted of, as reported by the author?

3. What sort of problems does ConsumerLab.com discover in dietary supplements, according to president Tod Cooperman, as cited by Tsouderos?

Federal inspections of companies that make dietary supplements—from multivitamins and calcium chews to capsules of echinacea and bodybuilding powders—reveal serious and widespread manufacturing problems in a $28 billion industry that sells products consumed by half of all Americans.

In the last four years [2008–2012], the U.S. Food and Drug Administration [FDA] has found violations of manufacturing rules in half of the nearly 450 dietary supplement firms it has inspected, according to agency officials.

The inspection reports portray an industry struggling to meet basic manufacturing standards, from verifying the identity of the ingredients that go into its products to inspecting finished batches of supplements.

Some firms don't even have recipes, known as master manufacturing records, for their products.

Multiple Violations

Others make their supplements in unsanitary factories. New Jersey–based Quality Formulation Laboratories produced protein powder mixes and other supplements in a facility infested with rodents, rodent feces and urine, according to government records. FDA inspectors found a rodent apparently cut in half next to a scoop, according to a 2008 inspection report.

"It's downright scary," said Daniel Fabricant, head of the FDA's Division of Dietary Supplement Programs. "At least half of industry is failing on its face."

The FDA began conducting inspections in 2008 to assess compliance with new regulations governing the manufacturing, packing and holding of dietary supplements. Since then, 1 in 4 dietary supplement companies inspected by the agency have received a warning letter, considered a significant enforcement action.

So far this year [2012], FDA inspectors have found violations of good manufacturing practices during two-thirds of the 204 inspections they have conducted in nearly 200 supplement firms' facilities, agency officials said. Seventy of these inspections resulted in the agency's most serious rating.

Significant Efforts to Comply

Cara Welch, vice president of scientific and regulatory affairs for the Natural Products Association, a large dietary supplement trade group based in Washington, D.C., called the inspection numbers "unfortunate" and a significant issue her organization has been tackling.

"We can't give up on the industry," Welch said. "We are going to make it as strong as can be."

Manufacturers large and small are making significant efforts to implement the regulations, including sections borrowed from the FDA's drug manufacturing rules, said Michael McGuffin, president of the American Herbal Products Association, a trade association based in Silver Spring, Md.

But it takes time for companies to come into compliance with such a large and complex set of rules and for the FDA to establish how the rules will be enforced, McGuffin said. "Not everybody was in compliance on the day the rule was passed, but that is not uncommon in any rulemaking," he said.

Fabricant disagreed. The final rule was published in 2007. "You can get a lot done in five years," he said.

Health Issues

Underscoring the importance of the issue, some customers have suffered serious health problems linked to companies' poor manufacturing practices.

In 2008 more than 200 people—including a 4-year-old—were poisoned by selenium after taking liquid multivitamin dietary supplements that were sold in health stores and by chiropractors, according to a medical paper published on the mass poisoning. The products, called Total Body Formula and Total Body Mega Formula, contained an average of 40,800 micrograms of selenium per serving instead of 200, according to the paper.

John Adams, of Chipley, Fla., was one of the victims. His silver hair—which had earned him the nickname "Silvertop" at work—began falling out in clumps. His fingernails and toenails became discolored, peeled off, regrew and peeled off again. He had a hard time remembering how to do his job as a telephone repairman. He became so weak it was hard to get in and out of his work truck, and eventually he was forced to retire.

Adams and his wife, who also experienced problems, sued along with dozens of others. This year, the couple received a settlement. Adams, now 65, said he is still weak on his left side, has ruined fingernails and toenails that do not grow and struggles with memory problems.

"What is a person in America to do to be healthy?" Adams wrote in an email. "Who can you trust? Not the supplement industry because it does not take long for a tainted product to make you very sick."

Rod Cate, attorney for Total Body Essential Nutrition, the distributor of the products, wrote in an email that his client had been in business for more than 10 years with no problems and with satisfied customers before the companies that manufactured Total Body Formula produced the tainted bottles.

In his opinion, Cate wrote, the problem was caused by contractors incorrectly interpreting the formula, incorrectly formulating it, or both. The company is in the midst of settling lawsuits, he wrote.

Warning Letters

"Not sure if FDA inspections of manufacturing facilities would have made any difference as this was a problem with formulation and not a problem with the manufacturing facilities themselves," Cate wrote.

Fabricant called the Total Body Formula incidents "a classic case" of not adhering to good manufacturing practices. "This is why these things are important," he said.

Unlike drug companies, dietary supplement firms are not required by law to prove to the FDA that their products work or are safe before they sell them. The FDA does regulate the claims that firms make about their products—for example, companies cannot say a supplement will cure a disease—and the agency can take action if it deems a product to be an imminent hazard or significant risk.

The FDA also can regulate the way supplements are made, and in 2008, the agency began enforcing its new rules through inspections of the largest of the industry's nearly 1,400 supplement firms. Medium-sized and small firms were given a year or two longer to comply.

A flurry of warning letters soon followed, along with more serious consequences like legal action against companies and their owners.

In the case of the Paterson, N.J., supplement plant infested with rodents, the federal government filed a civil complaint against Quality Formulation Laboratories, related companies and their owner in 2009. The defendants agreed to stop manufacturing and distributing their products and to meet a series of conditions before starting up again.

Instead, according to the government, the defendants simply moved their production to another plant in Congers, N.Y., even providing transportation to the facility for employees. Last year [2011], a jury found the defendants guilty of multiple counts of criminal contempt, fining the companies and sentencing the owners and managers to prison time. The convictions are being appealed.

Bradford Williams, manager of the FDA Division of Dietary Supplement Programs, expressed exasperation while addressing an audience at SupplySide West, a large dietary supplement conference in Las Vegas in October [2011].

A Steep Learning Curve

"It doesn't seem that the firms are getting it," Williams said. "How do I reach this industry? Do I have to use nuclear bombers to do it?"

McGuffin's response: "I understand from (Williams') point of view he wants it all to be perfect right now. But that's not the real world." Other industries have experienced steep learning curves—with similar or worse violation rates—when government introduces new regulations, he said.

"I don't excuse the industry for not being prepared, but I would expect there would be a higher level of out-of-spec issues on that first go-round," said Steve Mister, president of the Council for Responsible Nutrition, a dietary supplement and ingredient supplier trade association based in Washington, D.C. "In many cases, the companies are learning as the inspector is there."

Fabricant said the FDA's rules are basic and often cover practices—like ensuring the finished product matches specifications—that should have been in place long ago. Warning letters typically are sent after firms fail to fix problems identified in earlier inspections, he said.

In one typical example, an Eden Prairie, Minn., company called Milk Specialties Global got an FDA warning letter in December [2011] after an inspection of its plant in Wautoma, Wis. According to the letter, the plant did not establish specifications for finished batches of some supplements—such as what exactly should be in the products.

The agency also said the company kept incomplete records of its batches of supplements and failed to record how it makes decisions when changes are made during the production process.

In a statement, Milk Specialties Global spokeswoman Amy Rotenberg wrote that the company takes quality assurance and compliance with federal regulations very seriously. After getting the warning letter, the company sent the FDA detailed information about how it is complying with the rules.

"Milk Specialties is committed to continuing its ongoing best practices of manufacturing products of the highest quality and will continue to work cooperatively with the FDA," Rotenberg wrote.

In November, the FDA sued a Pennsylvania supplement manufacturer, ATF Fitness, its distributor and the two companies' owner after inspections reported the factory had substituted ingredients without changing product labels and did not have master recipes for its products, among other issues.

ATF Fitness, which produces more than 400 dietary supplements, also failed to investigate or to report to the FDA a serious health incident in which a customer claimed to have been hospitalized with a spike in blood pressure and a mild heart attack after allegedly ingesting a product called Kreation Powder, according to the complaint.

Michael DiMaggio, an attorney representing ATF Fitness, said the company has agreed not to manufacture, prepare, pack, label, hold or distribute any dietary supplement products until the FDA finds it to be in compliance. ATF Fitness also agreed to destroy any supplements in its possession that were not manufactured in accordance with current good manufacturing practices, he said.

Fear of a Public Health Catastrophe

The big worry, Fabricant said, is that lax controls by dietary supplement makers will cause a public health catastrophe.

In 2006, an ingredient mix-up killed more than 200 people in Panama and left many more sickened or disabled. In that tragedy, a Panamanian government pharmaceutical company failed to verify that a sweet syrup from China was glycerin, the ingredient it had ordered, according to a World Health Organization report.

It wasn't glycerin, the report said—it was diethylene glycol, a poison. Testing the identity of the ingredient would have revealed that.

ConsumerLab.com, an independent group based in White Plains, N.Y., has been unearthing problems with commercial dietary supplements through laboratory testing for a dozen years.

About 1 in 4 products the company tests have a significant problem, said Tod Cooperman, president of ConsumerLab.com. Some contain significantly less of an ingredient than is promised on the label, some far more. Sometimes the product contains contaminants, like lead. Some are rancid. Some have the correct ingredients but are "bedpan bullets"—incorrectly formulated pills that won't break up in the body.

The problems turn up in products from companies large and small, fringe and mainstream, Cooperman said.

Kirkman Labs, a maker of supplements popular among parents of children with autism, began a voluntary recall of 15,000 bottles of zinc and other products in late 2009. Although the company had boasted of its quality manufacturing, FDA documents reported that some of the company's products contained undeclared antimony, a heavy metal.

After customers' physicians reported that lab tests found unusual levels of antimony in their patients, Kirkman discovered that the metal was present in two lots of a sweetener, stevia leaf extract, used in the products, according to a letter the company posted on its website.

Melissa Cook, of Houma, La., had been giving her 11-year-old son Shawn a nightly dose of Kirkman's liquid zinc since March 2009, according to court records. Shawn, who has autism spectrum disorder, soon began having health problems, and a lab test showed an unusual level of antimony, records state. Cook is suing Kirkman, and a jury trial is set for next year.

"I think everybody was working on the assumption that anything that went into those supplements was being tested, especially because of this patient population," said attorney Ben Mouton, who is representing Cook and her son in the lawsuit. "You would think that there would be the same oversight as prescription drug manufacturers, but there is not."

The company declined to comment on Cook's case, citing ongoing litigation. But Kirkman CEO and President David Humphrey wrote in an email that the company has been working diligently to prevent this from happening again.

"We now test every raw ingredient in every product we manufacture (except lotions, creams and oils) for more than 900 environmental contaminants," Humphrey wrote. "This is a higher standard for purity testing than any other nutraceutical company we know of."

Toxicologists say that little is known about the effects of chronic antimony exposure on children, and that knowing the dose is key. But the company has not disclosed how much antimony was in the supplements, leaving parents in the dark, Mouton said.

Kirkman was a trusted supplier of supplements, one Cook and her son's physician believed in, he said. "It was a slap in the face," Mouton said, "a violation of trust."

> *"Medical professionals should be aware of the important qualitative and quantitative differences between the FDA-approved prescription formulations and dietary supplements."*

Doctors Must Be Aware of Different Regulations for Prescription Drugs and Dietary Supplements

Nancy Collins, Ann P. Tighe, Stephen A. Brunton, and Penny M. Kris-Etherton

The authors are all biomedical scientists who advise pharmaceutical companies. In the following viewpoint, they argue that prescription medication is safer and more efficacious than dietary supplements in many instances. In particular, they contend that dietary supplements of omega-3 fatty acid formulations do not reduce risks of heart disease as effectively as prescription omega-3 fatty acids.

Nancy Collins, Ann P. Tighe, Stephen A. Brunton, and Penny M. Kris-Etherton, "Differences Between Dietary Supplement and Prescription Drug Omega-3 Fatty Acid Formulations: A Legislative and Regulatory Perspective," *Journal of the American College of Nutrition*, vol. 27, December 2008, pp. 659–666. Copyright © 2008 by Taylor & Francis Informa UK LTD-Journals. All rights reserved. Reproduced by permission. Text has been altered from original version.

As you read, consider the following questions:

1. In patients with coronary heart disease, what is omega-3 fatty acid intake associated with, according to the authors?

2. What do the authors say are some dangers of St. John's wort?

3. What are the three phases of clinical trials, as described by the authors?

The medical management of many diseases and conditions can include either restriction or provision of specific essential nutrients. When such nutrients are needed, there are often both prescription and nonprescription products available, as in the case of nicotinic acid [a form of vitamin B_3] or omega-3 fatty acids. Although they may seem to contain similar ingredients, there may be important differences between the prescription and dietary-supplement preparations. The manufacturing of prescription pharmaceutical products is regulated by the US Food and Drug Administration (FDA), which mandates standards for consistency and quality assurance. Dietary supplements are available to consumers under the provisions of the Dietary Supplement Health and Education Act of 1994, for which the FDA has the burden of proving a dietary supplement is harmful rather than requiring the manufacturer prove that the supplement is safe. Consumers and medical professionals should be aware of the important qualitative and quantitative differences between the FDA-approved prescription formulations and dietary supplements, particularly when an essential nutrient is part of the medical management of a disease or condition.

Prescriptions and Supplements

- Prescription formulations, taken under a physician's supervision, are preferred when provision of a nutrient(s) are part of the medical management of a disease or condition.

- Fish or fish oil intake is positively associated with favorable cardiovascular outcomes. In patients with coronary heart disease, intake of omega-3 fatty acids is associated with reduced risk for overall mortality, mortality from myocardial infarction, and sudden death.

- There are qualitative and quantitative differences between FDA-approved prescription formulations and dietary supplements of omega-3 fatty acids.

- Omega-3-acid ethyl esters ([under the brand names] P-OM3; LOVAZA® capsules) is a lipid-lowering agent to be used in conjunction with diet for the reduction of severe hypertriglyceridemia [high blood fat levels] in adults [which causes a predisposition to heart disease].

Nutrition as Medicine

The medical management of many conditions, including diabetes, dyslipidemia, celiac disease, and heart disease, is intimately linked to nutrition. However, one of the challenges that has emerged is how best to utilize the various formulations of essential nutrients within the paradigm of an evidence-based practice of medicine. While dietary-supplement forms of many nutrients may help promote well being and even mitigate the risk for certain types of diseases, their use may not be safe or effective as part of the medical management of a disease. Although the regulation of dietary supplements has grown more stringent over the decades, there remains a great deal of misinformation, among both consumers and medical professionals. What are the differences between dietary supplements and prescription formulations of essential nutrients, and what is the basis for these differences?

Prescription formulations, taken under a physician's supervision, are preferred when nutrients are indicated for the treatment of a disease or condition. . . .

More than 115 million Americans use dietary supplements, with sales exceeding $17 billion in 2000. Many consumers and medical professionals are unaware that the contents of dietary supplements are not regulated by any agency at this time, and they can vary widely depending on the manufacturer and its standards. Although there are both prescription and dietary supplement formulations available, governmental regulation, oversight, and quality-assurance processes are quite different. The preparation, packing, and holding of dietary supplements under safe conditions is governed by the FDA's "Good Manufacturing Practices" (GMPs). However, the GMPs applicable to dietary supplements are those used for foods, not for drugs. The FDA recently established revised GMP regulations that require dietary supplement manufacturers ". . . to evaluate the identity, purity, strength, and composition of their dietary supplements." Mandatory compliance with these regulations will take effect between June 2008 and June 2010. Manufacturers of prescription drugs undergo rigorous evaluation of compliance with processing of active pharmaceutical ingredients. The FDA Compliance Program Manual is a guide for evaluating compliance with GMPs and provides comprehensive regulatory coverage of production and distribution of active pharmaceutical ingredients to ensure compliance with the Federal Food, Drug, and Cosmetic (FD&C) Act. . . . The purpose of this viewpoint is to review the clinically relevant differences between dietary supplement and prescription formulations of omega-3 fatty acids in the context of legislative and regulatory issues.

DSHEA: Friend or Foe?

Food and drug regulation in the United States began in the late 19th century, when both state and federal governments began to enact laws with the intent of protecting consumers and providing uniform expectations for producers. The FD&C Act of 1938 compelled manufacturers to demonstrate to the FDA the safety of new drugs before marketing. DSHEA [Dietary Supplement Health and Education Act] was designed to ensure that safe and appropriately labeled products remain available to those who choose to use them.

The DSHEA amendment was passed to allow the public access to information regarding dietary supplements. However, consumers and medical professionals may confront problems as a result of this act. Patients may perceive dietary supplements to be appropriate substitutes for prescription medication, or they may not consult with, or inform health-care professionals about, their dietary supplement use. Also, there may be a perception that dietary supplements are harmless. This is not the case. For example, St. John's wort (*Hypericum perforatum*), a popular dietary supplement used by some consumers as a putative herbal antidepressant, can attenuate [lessen] the efficacy of prescription medications. Moreover, a growing body of evidence indicates that high doses of some dietary supplement vitamins may increase morbidity or mortality in certain patient populations. For example, a recent meta-analysis of antioxidant supplements in primary and secondary prevention trials suggests that treatment with beta carotene, vitamin A, and vitamin E may increase all-cause mortality. In 2004, the FDA prohibited the sale of [the herb] ephedra in the United States due to the risk of stroke, cardiac arrhythmia, and death associated with use of dietary supplements that contained ephedra. This is an extreme example of adverse events, but evaluating products intended to take ephedra's place in the market does illustrate the general lack of safety and efficacy data within the dietary-supplement industry. Problems may arise when these products are of inconsistent quality and are not taken under the supervision of medical professionals.

Prescription-Drug Regulation

Before a prescription drug is approved for a disease or condition, it undergoes rigorous review by the FDA. Prior to initiating clinical testing of new products, companies must submit an investigational new drug (IND) application or investigational new animal drug application. The IND becomes effective within 1 month unless the FDA places a clinical hold on the application or on the clinical trial once in progress because it finds deficiencies such as concerns about the qualifications of the researchers.

Preclinical studies provide safety data and help establish if the drug should proceed to clinical testing. The IND will specify how the sponsoring company, institution, and researcher plan to further investigate the safety of the drug in human subjects and discuss the toxicologic and pharmacologic data obtained in preclinical studies. Treatment INDs permit companies to make drugs available to patients who are not part of clinical trials if the drugs are intended to treat serious illnesses such as AIDS and trials are currently in progress.

Clinical Trials

There are 3 phases of clinical trials. Phase I trials help determine how a drug is metabolized, help establish the optimal dose, and usually involve fewer than 100 people. These studies may help researchers gauge the proper dose of the product. Phase II trials explore the safety and effectiveness of the product as well as side effects and may involve hundreds of patients. Early phase II studies may try to assess the efficacy of the drug, while later studies may evaluate how much better (if at all) the drug is than a placebo given to patients with similar conditions and characteristics. If these studies indicate that the drug is effective, phase III trials, which examine the long-term safety and efficacy of the product and often involve thousands of patients, may begin. These pivotal studies are designed to gather the information needed to gain FDA approval. The FDA has issued many guidelines related to the conduct of clinical trials and may meet with sponsors during the clinical trial process.

Clinical trials must be conducted in accordance with the FDA's Good Clinical Practice rules, a series of regulations published by the FDA, which require institutional review boards (IRBs) to review clinical study protocols, informed consent from subjects, and monitoring. The FDA's Office for Good Clinical Practice monitors clinical trial issues and helps set the agency's policies on these issues, working with the department's Office of Human Research Protection. Although the Bioresearch Monitoring program inspects clinical trial sponsors, IRBs and investigators can reject studies, halt studies, disqualify sponsors or researchers from working on studies, and send warning letters or take other enforcement action against facilities or individuals that fail to comply with Good Clinical Practices. Most trials involving new drugs are funded by pharmaceutical companies, which hire clinical study coordinators and monitors to ensure that FDA regulations are followed or pay contract research organizations to monitor the studies. An industry trade group, Pharmaceutical Research and Manufacturers of America (PhRMA), has published voluntary guidelines spelling out the obligations of companies conducting trials to protect patients, minimize conflicts of interest among clinical investigators, and adequately monitor trials and publish results.

The Case of Omega-3 Fatty Acids

A myriad of health benefits have been attributed to increased consumption of omega-3 fatty acids. In particular, fish or fish oil intake is positively associated with favorable cardiovascular outcomes. . . . Recognition of the potential cardioprotective effects of omega-3 fatty acids can be traced to the observation that indigenous populations [that is, native peoples] consuming high concentrations of [the Omega-3 fatty acids] EPA and DHA (eg, marine mammals and fatty fish) have low rates of coronary heart disease. In patients with coronary heart disease, intake of omega-3 fatty acids is associated with reduced risk for overall mortality, mortality from myocardial infarction, sudden death and all-cause death or admission to hospital for cardiovascular reasons in patients with chronic heart failure. European and American cardiac societies include EPA and DHA in recent treatment guidelines for myocardial infarction, prevention of cardiovascular disease, treatment of ventricular arrhythmias, and prevention of sudden cardiac death. The recent AHA [American Heart Association] guidelines for women state that, as an adjunct to diet, omega-3 fatty acids in capsule form (approximately 0.85 to 1 g[ram] of EPA and DHA) may be considered in women with coronary heart disease.

The omega-3 fatty acids EPA and DHA have been shown to reduce triglyceride [blood fat] levels in a wide range of patient types. According to the AHA guidelines for women, omega-3 fatty acids in capsule form at doses of 2 to 4 g/day may be used as an adjunct to diet for the treatment of high triglyceride levels. Importantly, the AHA indicates that treatment with these dosages of omega-3 fatty acids be taken only under physician supervision. . . .

In general, dietary supplement omega-3 fatty acids contain only modest concentrations of EPA and DHA. An independent analysis of 41 omega-3 fatty acid dietary supplements found that most products met label claims, although the contents of one product were spoiled, while a second dietary supplement omega-3 product contained only 53% of its claimed EPA content. Dietary supplement omega-3 fatty acids typically do not contain toxins, such as mercury, polychlorinated biphenyls, dioxin, and other contaminants, in sufficient concentrations to pose a potential health risk. However, some dietary-supplement omega-3 fatty acids, at amounts attempting to achieve EPA and DHA content approximating that of four P-OM3 capsules, require the use of up to 18 capsules daily. This has important clinical implications, as the quantity of prescribed medications may be inversely correlated with patient compliance. Thus, the high concentrations of omega-3-acid ethyl esters in P-OM3 may foster better patient compliance compared with less-concentrated formulations.

Oversight and Verification Is Necessary

In 2001 the United States Pharmacopeial Convention, Inc. (USP), a nongovernmental, nonprofit organization, launched a verification program for dietary supplements. This program assures consumers that a dietary supplement bearing the USP verification mark has accurate ingredient labeling and follows USP-verified GMPs. Although the USP verification program does not accept dietary supplements that contain an ingredient with known safety concerns, it does not comprehensively address issues of safety and efficacy. Data on the efficacy and safety of dietary supplement omega-3 fatty acids may be lacking, insufficient, or inconsistent. One study, the diet and reinfarction trial (DART), showed that subjects advised to eat fatty fish had a 29% reduction in 2-year all-cause mortality compared with subjects not given dietary advice. Notably, subjects who took a fish oil supplement as a partial or total substitute for fatty fish showed the same benefit as subjects who ate fatty fish. In addition, the FDA-Qualified Health Claim for dietary supplements that contain omega-3 fatty acids does offer some oversight for safety concerns.

The efficacy and safety of P-OM3 for the treatment of hypertriglyceridemia has been studied extensively in clinical trials. The recommended daily dosage of P-OM3 is 4 g/day, taken as a single dose of 4 capsules or 2 divided doses of 2 capsules. Claims that a dietary supplement omega-3 fatty acid product is "pharmaceutical grade" do not reflect credible safety and efficacy data unless the product is approved by the FDA as a prescription pharmaceutical. Importantly, patients should discuss the choice of treatment of hypertriglyceridemia with a qualified health professional. At this time, P-OM3 is the only FDA-approved omega-3 fatty acid formulation for the treatment of hypertriglyceridemia.

Important Differences

There are important qualitative and quantitative differences between the FDA-approved P-OM3 and dietary supplement omega-3 fatty acids. Both consumers and medical professionals should be aware that dietary supplement omega-3 fatty acids may not have the same efficacy and safety profile as P-OM3. Notably, the efficacy and safety of P-OM3 have been demonstrated in randomized, placebo-controlled trials. The FDA has advised that no more than 2 g/day of EPA and DHA be provided by dietary supplements. Effective dosages of EPA and DHA for the treatment of hypertriglyceridemia should be undertaken only under a physician's care.

> *"Regulations . . . in the [European Union] regarding the sale of herbal products . . . seem reasonable."*

European Union Regulations on Herbal Dietary Supplements Are Reasonable and Necessary

Steven Novella

Steven Novella is a clinical neurologist and an assistant professor at Yale University. In the following viewpoint, he argues that the European Union's new regulations relating to dietary supplements are reasonable and necessary. He contends that dietary supplements can have dangerous effects and that consumers have the right to know whether the products they purchase are safe. He also contends that the licensing fees for dietary supplements are not exorbitant by the standards of the industry's wealth. He concludes that it is reasonable that substances that act like drugs be regulated like drugs.

As you read, consider the following questions:

1. According to Novella, what is required for an herbal product to be licensed under the new European regulations?

2. Why does Novella say that the FDA (Food and Drug Administration) wants to put mom-and-pop patent-medicine sellers out of business?

3. Why is there a disincentive to do good efficacy research on supplements, according to the author?

Regulations have just gone into effect in the EU [European Union] regarding the sale of herbal products. The regulations seem reasonable, but they have sparked near hysteria on the part of herbal sellers and advocates of "natural" medicine. They are calling the regulation a "ban" on herbal products, which much of the media has parroted, but it is not a true ban, just a requirement for registration.

Marketing Freedom vs. Quality Control

The law was sparked by cases of toxicity from over-the-counter herbal products. For example, aristolochia is a toxic plant species that is either used deliberately or can be accidentally or carelessly substituted for other plant species. It is known to cause kidney damage—even leading to kidney failure is some cases. Another herb, kava, has been linked to liver damage.

The new EU law, which went into effect May 1, 2011, will require herbal products to be licensed, or prescribed by a licensed herbal practitioner. In order to be licensed, evidence for safety of the product must be presented. It is estimated that it will cost between 80,000 and 120,000 British pounds [US$131,710 and US$197,566] to get an individual herbal product licensed.

I find it interesting, and completely predictable, that sellers of herbal products are wailing that this is all a conspiracy by "Big Pharma" to crush the little guy and steal all the herbal profits for themselves, or to ban herbal products to protect their drug profits. But this is a straw man [an illogical argument]. The real question here is the balance between marketing freedom and quality control—but those who want to defend their right to sell herbs don't want to discuss the real issues, apparently.

Dr Rob Verkerk from a trade organization, the ANH [Alliance for Natural Health], is quoted as saying:

"Thousands of people across Europe rely on herbal medicines to improve their quality of life. They don't take them because they are sick—they take them to keep healthy. If these medicines are taken off the market, people will try and find them elsewhere, such as from the internet, where there is a genuine risk they will get low quality products, that either don't work or are adulterated."

First, he begs the question that the use of herbs improves anyone's quality of life. That is, in fact, the entire question—are the risks worth the alleged benefits. The legislation is simply an attempt to provide a better risk/benefit for the consumer by putting into play better assurances of safety.

His next point is the same point that is always made against regulation—if you make X illegal then people will just obtain X illegally or from less regulated sources. This is not specific to herbal products. There is a point there—regulation is not easy, especially with a global market and the internet. But that does not mean we should abandon all efforts at quality control and honesty in marketing.

He concludes with an assumption that herbal products under the current scheme work for anything and have adequate quality control—but again, that is the very issue. In fact regulations are generally not adequate to assure quality control in terms of dose and purity. And there is virtually no regulation about the claims that can be made for herbal products.

Bans on the Herb Kava

The Federal Institute of Germany has withdrawn all products that contain kava and kavaine from the German market because of the risk of hepatotoxicity [liver poisoning] and insufficiently proven efficacy.... The German regulation applies to all kava-containing pharmaceutical formulations. Moreover, following a provisional opinion from the UK Committee on Safety of Medicine (CSM), the Medicines and Healthcare products Regulatory Agency (MHRA) has consulted on a proposal to prohibit the sale, supply, or importation of unlicensed medicinal products containing kava in the UK. The CSM reviewed the issue of kava-associated liver toxicity following the emergence of safety concerns in Europe. At that time, stocks of kava were voluntarily withdrawn by the herbal sector while the safety concerns were under investigation. Currently the MHRA is aware of 68 cases worldwide of suspected kava-associated liver problems, including 6 cases of liver failure that resulted in transplant, and 3 deaths. The CSM has advised consumers to stop taking medicinal products containing kava, and to seek medical advice if they feel unwell or have concerns about possible liver problems.

Kava has been associated with toxic liver damage in six cases reported from Switzerland. In one patient, the liver damage was so extensive that liver transplantation became necessary.... The leading kava extract, Laitan, was subsequently withdrawn from the Swiss market.

Australia's Therapeutic Goods Administration initiated a voluntary recall of all complementary medicines containing kava after the death of a woman who used a medicine containing kava.

J.K. Aronson, ed.
Meyler's Side Effects of Herbal Medicines, 2009.

Not Far Enough

In the US the 1994 DSHEA [Dietary Supplement Health and Education Act] essentially allows herbal manufacturers to make a host of pseudo-health claims without any oversight. The same is and will continue to be true in the EU. One could argue that this legislation does not go far enough to protect the public against false claims and useless products.

Others argue that this legislation will put the small producers out of business. This is exactly what patent medicine sellers complained about when the FDA was proposed. In fact all of the objections are identical to those raised against regulation of drugs. Of course, the point of the FDA was to put the mom and pop patent medicine sellers out of business—because they were largely selling snake oil and did not have the resources to perform proper safety and efficacy testing.

Here the claims are even less relevant—because herbal remedies are a multi-billion dollar industry, and the relative cost to get licensing is much less than getting a drug through the FDA.

What we really have here is an industry that wants to continue selling poorly regulated products with health claims and without any burden of having to prove that their products are safe or that their health claims are based upon science.

I acknowledge that there is a real political debate here, and that some people might want to favor freedom and risk over government regulation. But I object to the way the debate is often framed by opponents to regulation. Even those who would prefer to have a free market for herbal products would likely agree that the consumer deserves accurate information in order to make informed decisions. Right now, in most markets, the consumer does not have that.

Freedom and Protection

Most people I talk to about this assume that herbs are more regulated than they currently are. People want both freedom and protection, and are not always aware of the degree to which the two are at cross purposes. So if you ask them if they want freedom in the market, they say yes. And if you ask them if they want assurance of safety and honesty, they also say yes. They want the freedom to choose, but only among products that are safe and effective.

With respect to herbal remedies, however, the evidence is largely against the efficacy that is being claimed for many products. If you look at the big sellers, like echinacea and Gingko biloba, the large well-controlled studies are largely negative—they don't appear to work for the indications for which they are commonly marketed.

The industry has largely failed to self-regulate, and to use their profits to generate good science to back up their claims. And they consistently fight against regulation to force them to do so, and try to make it seem like they are on the side of the little guy against big corporate interests. But this is just spin— they are just another big industry protecting their interests. If they really cared about the little guy or the consumer they would be producing good science, and keeping their claims within the evidence, rather than fighting against attempts to make them do just that.

Under most current regulatory schemes, there is a disincentive to conduct good efficacy research. Such research is a lose-lose proposition for industry. They have to spend the money to do the research. If it's positive, it is unclear how that will benefit them since they already can make health claims (or pseudo-health claims, like the so-called "structure function" claims under DSHEA).[1] But if it's negative, then they risk losing market share. The risk/benefit of doing efficacy research is simply not there, and that is probably why there is so little such industry-sponsored research into supplements. The

---

1. Claims about how a supplement affects normal structures or functions in individuals. These claims are not approved, but may not be misleading.

only way to get the industry to spend some of their profits doing quality research is to make such research a requirement for entry into the marketplace.

In the end we should remember that herbs are drugs—they have pharmacological activity, they have toxicity, and they have drug-drug interactions. How much regulation and quality assurance do we want for our drug industries (no matter what they are called)?

> "Herbalists and nutritionists have spoken of their fears that the new European Union rules, which have been introduced under the banner of patient safety, will do more harm than good."

European Union Regulations on Herbal Dietary Supplements Are Unreasonable and Dangerous

WalesOnline

WalesOnline is a website in the United Kingdom. In the following viewpoint, it argues that new European Union rules on herbal medicines will hurt consumers without improving safety. The author contends that there are concerns that forcing herbs to be licensed will drive prices up, putting them beyond the reach of some consumers and perhaps forcing some herbs off the market altogether. The author maintains that consumers may then shop for herbs online, which may well be less safe.

As you read, consider the following questions:

1. What conditions must herbs meet in order to be licensed under the new European Union (EU) rules, according to the author?

2. Why does Paul Gimson, as cited by WalesOnline, say that the new licensing rules could be confusing for consumers?

3. What does the author provide as examples of herbs that will no longer be stocked in health food stores under the new regulations?

New rules on herbal medicines could compromise patient safety by forcing people to turn to the internet to buy their supplies.

Herbalists and nutritionists have spoken of their fears that the new European Union rules, which have been introduced under the banner of patient safety, will do more harm than good.

The EU directive on herbal medicines, which came into force in the UK at the start of May [2011], could see common and popular remedies removed from shop shelves.

Under the rules, over-the-counter herbal medicine products must be licensed—in the UK they require either a Traditional Herbal Medicines Registration (THR) or a full marketing authorisation. To be eligible for a licence products must have been on the market for 30 years, including 15 within the EU.

To date 100 herbal products have been registered under the THR scheme, which is run by the Medicines and Healthcare products Regulatory Agency (MHRA).

Richard Woodfield, the MHRA's head of herbal medicine policy, said: "The growth of the THR scheme means that consumers will have access to a wide choice of over-the-counter herbal medicines made to assured standards.

"The current signs are that the market will be lively and competitive. The key difference for consumers is that in the future they will be in the driving seat and able to make an informed choice when they wish to use these medicines."

Paul Gimson, director of the Royal Pharmaceutical Society in Wales, said the full implementation of the directive was a "positive step".

But he added: "Whereas ibuprofen, for example, has to prove it cures pain, herbal remedies do not have to prove they work—only that they've been used as a traditional remedy.

"This could be confusing for patients when buying something—making claims based on tradition is not the same as claims made by medicines based on clinical trials."

A Public Outcry

Support for the new EU rules is by no means universal—an online petition by campaign group Avaaz, which calls on the European Commission to overturn the "ban" on herbal medicines, has already been signed by more than 750,000 people.

Dr Nicola Gale, academic lead for the Complementary and Alternative Medicine Birmingham Research Alliance, said: "The rationale behind the EU directive is persuasive—there are some safety risks with herbs because of their strong action or potential interaction with conventional pharmaceutical drugs.

"However, herbs are the 'traditional' medicine of the West—they are part of our heritage and have been used for many centuries to manage everything from minor health complaints to serious illness.

"The idea that people would have to consult their doctor to get access to these herbs or that there would be a dramatic restriction on the herbs available has caused widespread outcry across Europe with accusations of promoting a nanny state, restricting individual choice and playing into the hands of pharmaceutical companies seeking profits from patenting herbal treatments."

Vicky Perks, a clinical nutritionist for The Health Diva and the Beanfreaks chain of health food stores, said: "No matter what anyone says, this is not about safety—safety is already in place for consumers.

"If you buy anything from a shop it's governed by consumer law; everything in that product must be safe for human consumption.

"There's a reprieve for anyone who goes to a licensed medical herbalist but Chinese medicines are not covered—do we really know what's in those jars of medicines?

"I'd appreciate tighter legislation on certain areas but this legislation is so poorly thought out."

She added: "It would have been a better idea if they said the companies making these products had to be licensed rather than the product themselves.

Some Herbs Will Disappear

"Licensing is just a way of generating extra money for the government. It costs £50,000 to license one product—that level of cost is all right for the pharmaceutical industry, which sells billions of a product as it equates to something like an extra penny on a medicine.

"But things aren't the same in this industry as many of the companies that make products are small and have small turnovers. Many will say they simply can't afford to do this."

The British Herbal Medicine Association believes at least 50 herbs, including horny goat weed (so-called natural Viagra), hawthorn berry, which is used to treat angina pain, and wild yam [used to balance hormone levels], will no longer be stocked in health food shops.

Some familiar preparations may also disappear to be replaced by alternative licensed formulas, which contain different ingredients—Ms Perks said she is unwilling to stock some products containing artificial colourings.

Liz Sanders, a [Welsh] herbalist . . . said: "These new rules take away personal choice and freedom of choice and because many products will no longer be available in health food shops people will turn to the internet—I wouldn't buy anything medical over the internet because you simply don't know what you are getting."

The MHRA has issued guidance to people about buying unlicensed herbal remedies online, saying: "The best advice for consumers when it comes to buying herbal medicines over the internet is to be alert and cautious.

"There is an international trade in poor-quality, unregulated and unlicensed herbal products. Some of these have been found to contain banned pharmaceutical ingredients or heavy metals, which are poisonous.

"Products may also contain harmful herbs that are not permitted in the UK, and you should be aware that unlicensed herbal medicines manufactured outside the UK may not be subject to any form of effective regulation."

Ms Sanders added: "These new regulations will really impact on those people who want to use herbal medicines but cannot afford the consultation fees to see a herbalist—this is particularly sad because herbal medicine has traditionally been a poor man's medicine.

"If people don't have the money to see a proper herbalist then they will try and do it themselves.

"While there are some pros for this approach, the overall effect is that this type of medicine is being pushed away from people when it should be on a par with orthodox medicine."

Periodical and Internet Sources Bibliography

The following articles have been selected to supplement the diverse views presented in this chapter.

Chicago Tribune	"Supplements: The Battle Over New Ingredients," September 9, 2011.
Europa	"Q&A: Registration of Traditional Herbal Medicines," April 2, 2011. http://europa.eu.
Food and Drug Administration	"Dietary Supplements," February 27, 2013. www.fda.gov.
Scott Gavura	"Supplement Regulation: Be Careful What You Wish For," Science-Based Medicine, August 5, 2010. www.sciencebasedmedicine.org.
Daniel Hannan	"EU Bans Herbal Remedies: Another Victory for Corporate Interests," *Daily Telegraph* (London), December 30, 2010.
Ofelia Hunter	"Dietary Supplements Could Cause More Harm than Benefit," *Alice (TX) Echo-News*, March 11, 2013.
Robin McKie	"Herbal Remedies Banned as New EU Rules Take Effect," *The Guardian* (Manchester, UK), April 20, 2011.
NBC News	"FDA Seizes Illegal Diet Supplements in Florida," February 14, 2013. www.nbcnews.com.
Felicia Stoler	"The Skinny on FDA Regulation of Dietary Supplements," Fox News, March 23, 2012. www.foxnews.com.
Courtney Zubowski	"Attorney: More Regulation Needed for Dietary Supplements," KENS5 San Antonio, December 23, 2010. www.kens5.com.

Are Vitamin and Mineral Supplements Beneficial?

Chapter Preface

In many countries, vitamin D supplements are highly recommended for pregnant women. For example, in the United Kingdom, the government has decided that vitamin D supplements are so important that they are provided free of charge to women who cannot afford them.

Why do doctors believe that pregnant women need to supplement vitamin D? Vitamin D helps to maintain the correct levels of calcium in the body. If a woman does not have enough calcium in her body while she is pregnant or breastfeeding, many doctors believe, her baby may have underdeveloped teeth or bones.

In most cases, people receive the vitamin D they need from sunlight. Since the United Kingdom is fairly far north of the equator in addition to having many cloudy days, many people who live there do not receive recommended levels of vitamin D. For that reason, doctors often suggest vitamin D supplementation.

A study published in the prestigious British medical journal *The Lancet*, however, in 2013 found that vitamin D supplements seem to have no effect on the development of fetal bones. Researcher Debbie Lawlor concluded that "We believe that there is no strong evidence that pregnant women should receive vitamin D supplementation to prevent low BMC [bone mineral content] in their offspring." So according to this study, at least, the British program to get all pregnant women to take vitamin D supplements is unnecessary.

Some studies have indicated that vitamin D supplements have other positive benefits for pregnant women, however. According to a May 1, 2010, article by Denise Mann on CNN.com, pregnant women could safely take ten times as much vitamin D as is usually included in supplements. Not only did researchers find that the increased dosage was safe, but that it decreased early labor and other complications during pregnancy.

So should women take vitamin D supplements during pregnancy? The answer is still unclear, and more research needs to be conducted. For the moment, women should consult their doctors for specific recommendations based on their diet, ethnicity, location, and habits.

The viewpoints in this chapter debate the efficacy of particular vitamins and mineral supplements for treating specific groups and conditions.

| "Dietary supplements, used sensibly, can help fill gaps in our diets."

Vitamins Can Be a Beneficial Dietary Supplement When Taken with Care

Jennifer LaRue Huget

Jennifer LaRue Huget is a columnist for the Health section of the Washington Post. In the following viewpoint, she contends that it is best for people to get their vitamins and minerals from food, because food includes fiber and other essentials for good health, but she argues that it is difficult for many people to get all of the recommended daily allowance of all nutrients from their diet. Therefore, she concludes, a multivitamin or other dietary supplements can be a useful way for people to fill in the gaps and ensure that they are getting all the nutrients they need.

As you read, consider the following questions:

1. According to Huget, on what understanding is the "food first" approach based?

2. What four nutrients do Robert Post single out as of most concern, as cited by the author?

3. Who especially requires folate, according to Huget?

In an ideal world, no one would need dietary supplements. Our balanced diets would provide all the vitamins, minerals and other nutrients our bodies need.

Alas, the world of American eating is far from ideal. And that, some nutrition experts and supplement advocates argue, is why we need dietary supplements.

The latest federal data show that more than half of U.S. adults use dietary supplements, mostly multivitamins. But do we really need all those pills?

The Federal Dietary Guidelines

Depends on whom you ask. The latest version of the federal Dietary Guidelines for Americans urges us to get our nutrients primarily from food:

"A fundamental premise of the Dietary Guidelines is that nutrients should come primarily from foods. Foods in nutrient-dense, mostly intact forms contain not only the essential vitamins and minerals that are often contained in nutrient supplements, but also dietary fiber and other naturally occurring substances that may have positive health effects."

This "food first" approach is based on the emerging understanding that our bodies may process nutrients in food differently from those supplied by supplements and that foods contain scores of compounds whose synergy may be what makes them good for us.

The document also points out that "sufficient evidence is not available to support a recommendation for or against the use of multivitamin/mineral supplements in the primary prevention of chronic disease for the healthy American population."

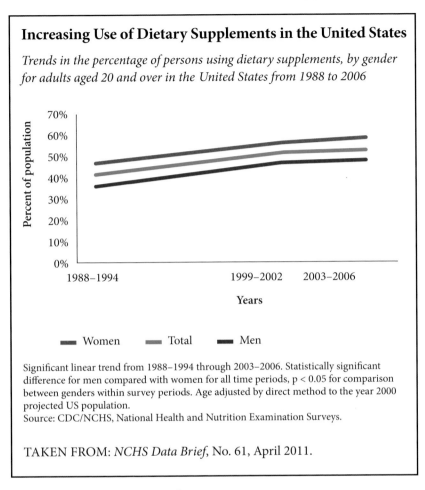

Increasing Use of Dietary Supplements in the United States

Trends in the percentage of persons using dietary supplements, by gender for adults aged 20 and over in the United States from 1988 to 2006

Significant linear trend from 1988–1994 through 2003–2006. Statistically significant difference for men compared with women for all time periods, p < 0.05 for comparison between genders within survey periods. Age adjusted by direct method to the year 2000 projected US population.
Source: CDC/NCHS, National Health and Nutrition Examination Surveys.

TAKEN FROM: *NCHS Data Brief*, No. 61, April 2011.

Supplements Fill In the Gaps

But . . . meeting your daily dietary needs without using supplements is a challenge, even when you're choosing ultra-healthful foods under a professional dietitian's guidance.

It's a widespread challenge. Society has "invested a lot in the science behind the Dietary Guidelines for Americans," says Duffy MacKay, vice president for scientific and regulatory affairs for the Council for Responsible Nutrition, a dietary supplement trade group. "When you think about people and what they're eating, a significant number are not meeting those benchmarks."

Robert Post, deputy director of the U.S. Department of Agriculture's [USDA's] Center for Nutrition Policy and Promotion, says too few Americans are meeting all their nutritional requirements and that dietary supplements, used sensibly, can help fill gaps in our diets. In particular, he notes, the guidelines single out four "nutrients of concern" that most of us need more of to maintain good health: potassium, Vitamin D, calcium and fiber.

But Post, like the guidelines, calls for people to get their fill of those four nutrients from food and to consider supplements only for a handful of dietary deficiencies related to our stage of life and dietary preferences. Those include:

Iron: Women who are able to become pregnant need more iron, especially heme iron, which the body absorbs more readily than non-heme iron. Heme iron is found in lean meat and poultry; non-heme iron is in white beans, lentils, spinach, enriched breads and cereals. Foods rich in Vitamin C can aid iron absorption. Adult males need just 8 mg of iron per day; women need 18 mg, and pregnant women need 27 mg.

Folate: Women who can bear children also should eat more foods containing folate, such as beans, peas, oranges, orange juice and dark-green leafy vegetables such as spinach, kale and mustard greens. Because folate and folic acid (the nutrient's synthetic form) help prevent neural-tube [spinal] defects in infants, women who can become pregnant should consume 400 micrograms of folic acid (from fortified foods or supplements); pregnant women should consume 600 mcg of folic acid daily.

Vitamin B_{12}: Some people aged 50 and older have trouble absorbing Vitamin B_{12} from food. To compensate, people 50 or older should increase consumption of cereals fortified with this vitamin or take supplements of it. Because B_{12} occurs naturally only in animal-based protein, vegetarians and vegans also should eat fortified cereals or take supplements. Most adults need 2.4 mcg per day.

Balanced Diet Plus a Multivitamin

Roberta Anding, director of sports nutrition at Texas Children's Hospital and a spokeswoman for the American Dietetic Association, advises consulting a physician or dietitian to determine the types and quantities of supplements that might benefit you. You can also consult the National Institutes of Health's Office of Dietary Supplements Web site (ods.od.nih.gov) for information, including potential interactions between supplements and medications. "Too much of a good thing is not a good thing," Anding says. "The dose determines whether it's beneficial or it's poison."

MacKay, whose job might seem to require him to push supplements over food, observes that good nutrition is "not an either-or situation."

"Focus on food first. Maintain a varied diet," MacKay suggests. "Once you take a snapshot of your diet, then figure out where to supplement to make sure you get everything you need."

The USDA is adamant that people try to get the fiber, potassium, Vitamin D and calcium they need by eating more fruits and vegetables. But the Harvard School of Public Health suggests a daily multivitamin, calling it "a great nutrition insurance policy."

MacKay agrees with that approach.

A multivitamin can smooth the "ups and downs of diet," he says. "It's not a magic bullet, and it's not promising anything, just filling in."

| "*Dietary supplements often don't have health benefits—and in some cases may even cause harm.*"

Is This the End of Popping Vitamins?

Shirley S. Wang

Shirley S. Wang is a health and science reporter for the Wall Street Journal. *In the following viewpoint, she asserts that more and more studies are showing that there is no benefit associated with taking vitamin supplements. Furthermore, she claims that some studies suggest that vitamin pills, such as vitamin C, are actually associated with a small increased risk of cancer. Wang says that more studies are needed because there is not really enough evidence to be sure that vitamins cause any increased risk to health. But she concludes there is mounting evidence that taking vitamin supplements is a waste of money.*

As you read, consider the following questions:

1. What are vitamins B-6 and B-12 supposed to do, according to Wang?

2. Who is Joseph Fortunato, as mentioned by the author?

3. What is the effect of beta-carotene on cancer rates, according to studies cited by Wang?

The case for dietary supplements is collapsing.

A succession of large-scale human studies, including two published earlier this month in leading medical journals, suggests that multivitamins and many other dietary supplements often don't have health benefits—and in some cases may even cause harm.

The data have prompted some nutrition researchers to say taking vitamins is a waste of money for those without a specific nutrient deficiency or chronic illness. Such findings have also fueled a debate about whether the field should continue conducting expensive human trials to figure out whether particular supplements affect health.

"The better the quality of the research, the less benefit [supplements] showed," says Marion Nestle, professor of nutrition, food studies, and public health at New York University. "It's fair to say from the research that supplements don't make healthy people healthier."

For instance, vitamins B-6 and B-12 are often touted as being good for the heart, but several studies have failed to find that they lower risk of cardiovascular disease, according the Office of Dietary Supplements, part of the National Institutes of Health. Vitamin C hasn't been shown in many studies to lower a person's risk of getting a cold. Calcium, while important to bone health, doesn't lower risk of heart disease or cancer and may increase risk of kidney stones.

"We have an enormous body of data telling us that plant-rich diets are very healthy," says Josephine Briggs, head of the National Center for Complementary and Alternative Medicine, another NIH center. "As soon as we take these various antioxidants [and other nutrients] out and put them in a pill, we're not consistently getting a benefit."

Potentially Harmful Vitamins for Cancer Patients

Vitamin A: Beta-carotene (which can be converted to vitamin A) and vitamin A have been shown in epidemiological studies to be associated with reduced cancer risk. However, a clinical trial (known as CARET) that evaluated these compounds in men and women smokers revealed that beta-carotene and vitamin A supplementation increased their rates of lung cancer and death from all causes. There have been no studies evaluating the safety of vitamin A supplementation following a diagnosis of breast cancer.

Vitamin E: Alpha-tocopherol (vitamin E) has been shown in epidemiological studies to be associated with reduced cancer risk. However, vitamin E supplementation has not been shown to reduce breast cancer risk in prospective trials and has been shown in multiple studies to increase risk of death due to all causes. Given no clear evidence of benefit, vitamin E supplementation is not recommended.

Barbara L. Gordon et al.,
Breast Cancer Recurrence and Advanced Disease, *2010.*

Researchers and nutritionists are still recommending dietary supplements for the malnourished or people with certain nutrient deficiencies or medical conditions. For instance folic acid—the supplement form of folate—reduces the likelihood of a common birth defect if taken by pregnant women.

Studying the effects of vitamins and supplements in the real world is difficult, since people eat foods with multiple nutrients that can interact with supplements and skew results. And observational trials can only show an association, not cause and effect.

That is one reason the Council on Responsible Nutrition, which represents the supplement industry, says it is too early to say supplements don't have health benefits. Duffy MacKay, the group's vice president of regulatory and scientific affairs, says lengthier studies may be required to show the benefits of some supplements.

Micronutrients, which include antioxidants like vitamin C, hormones like vitamin D and metals like iron, are essential to the body in small amounts because they help facilitate important reactions in and between cells. Too much of them, however, can cause problems.

The effectiveness of many dietary supplements remains untested and makers aren't required to do tests before selling a product. Still, about half of Americans reported taking at least one supplement a month in 2006, in the National Health and Nutrition Examination Survey published in April of this year. The supplement industry brought in $28 billion in sales in 2010, up 4.4% from 2009, according to *Nutrition Business Journal*, an industry trade publication.

Vitamin users may derive a benefit from the placebo effect, experts say. And they often are convinced the supplements make them feel better, regardless of what studies show.

"The thing you do with [reports of studies] is just ride them out, and literally we see no impact on our business," said Joseph Fortunato, chief executive of supplement retailer GNC Corp., according to a transcript of the company's third-quarter conference call with analysts last week.

"Consumers believe in our products," a spokesman for GNC said. GNC's revenue grew 15.5% in the third quarter of this year compared to a year ago and the stock, which closed at $25.08, is up 0.5% year-to-date.

Of growing concern to many scientists are the increasing hints of harm from vitamins.

The first red flags started emerging nearly 20 years ago. Researchers thought from early work that extra beta-carotene could help prevent lung cancer, but two randomized trials published in 1994 and 1996 showed an increased rate of lung cancer among smokers who took beta-carotene supplements.

Oncologist Mark Heaney of Memorial Sloan-Kettering Cancer Center in New York showed in laboratory work in 2008 that vitamin C appeared to inhibit the effect of chemotherapy drugs for cancer treatment. Subsequent research has shown vitamin C may inadvertently protect cancer cells more than normal cells.

A study published this month in the *Journal of the American Medical Association*, known as the SELECT trial, found that vitamin E—previously thought to lower risk of prostate cancer—actually increased the chance slightly. The risk could be mitigated by the simultaneous consumption of another micronutrient, selenium, the study says.

Multivitamins aren't faring much better. Results from the Iowa Women's Health Study, published earlier this month in the *Archives of Internal Medicine*, found in a sample of over 38,000 older women, multivitamin use over time was linked with a slight but statistically significant increased risk of earlier mortality.

A study of 1,900 men and women in 15 cities across Europe published in 2008 in the *European Journal of Nutrition* followed healthy elderly individuals for 10 years. Among smokers in the study, those who took multivitamins were more likely to die younger than smokers who didn't.

Another large trial examining postmenopausal women in the NIH's Women's Health Initiative found no discernible impact from taking a multivitamin on preventing breast, lung or colorectal cancer, cardiovascular disease or premature death, according to the 2009 study published in the *Archives of Internal Medicine*.

Some experts warn against overemphasizing the potential harm of multivitamins because it isn't clear how that statistical uptick in risk of death would translate into actual increased risk in real life.

The consistent failure to show benefits has led researchers at the National Center for Complementary and Alternative Medicine and elsewhere to call for more lab experiments and small-scale studies of how the nutrients work, after over a decade of pursuing large, clinical trials of particular supplements' effectiveness.

"We've missed a step," says Alan Kristal, a professor of epidemiology at the University of Washington who studies the links between diet and cancer. "We need to understand the mechanism by which these things are acting."

Roberta Anding, a nutritionist at Texas Children's Hospital in Houston, says some people need multivitamins and other supplements, but she is cautious about the risk from high doses of micronutrients. "It's no longer nutrition when the doses become high, it's pharmacology," she says.

The best way to get micronutrients is through a balanced diet, she says.

"If you're looking at this as, 'At least I'm [taking a multivitamin],' but you're not exercising or eating well, then it is a waste of money," says Ms. Anding, a spokeswoman for the American Dietetic Association, a research and advocacy group.

> "Believing, incorrectly, that you've done something healthy by taking a vitamin pill makes you more likely to take . . . risks with your health."

Vitamins Can Lead People to Take Health Risks

Ben Goldacre

Ben Goldacre is a British physician, academic, and science writer. In the following viewpoint, he reports on a series of studies that showed that people who believed that they were taking supplements that were good for them were more likely to engage in risky behavior, including smoking and eating badly. Goldacre points out that studies also show that many vitamin supplements have little if any effect on health. He concludes that taking vitamin pills may encourage people to live less healthy lives, which means that taking vitamins may actually have a detrimental effect on your health.

As you read, consider the following questions:

1. According to Goldacre, what is the "licensing effect"?

2. What does the author say that the Cochrane review on antioxidant vitamin pills found?

3. What does Goldacre say is the harm from quackery?

We all have irrational fears—flying is plainly scarier than getting in a car—and we all have odd rituals that we use to manage them. But what if we believed our own hype about these rituals and became cocksure, perhaps even harming ourselves?

The Licensing Effect

Here is a concrete example. In the study of risk perception, people talk about "the licensing effect": when you take a vitamin pill, for example, you think you've done something healthy and wholesome, so you permit yourself to eat more chips [french fries] and have a cigarette. It sounds like a nice idea, but a bit vague.

Two new experiments put flesh on these bones. Firstly, researchers took 74 undergraduates who were daily smokers and divided them into two groups at random. The first group were given a dummy pill, a placebo, and were told just that: you're in the control group, taking a dummy pill, with no active ingredient. The other participants were in the vitamin pill group: you've been given a vitamin pill, they were told.

But in fact, the researchers had lied. Everyone in the study got the same dummy pill, with no active ingredient. Half of them *thought* they'd had a health-giving vitamin pill, because the intention was to see whether people's health behaviours change if they think they've had a nice, healthy vitamin pill.

After the pills, they were given a survey to fill out. Because it was Taiwan, where lots of people smoke, they were told: "This survey will take you about one hour to finish ... you're allowed to smoke if you want."

The results were startling. Firstly, people who thought they'd had a vitamin pill gave different answers on the survey.

These featured questions from the excellently titled Adolescent Invulnerability Scale (which has been reasonably well validated elsewhere), such as "Special problems, getting an illness or disease, are not likely to happen to me", "I'm unlikely to be injured in an accident", and so on. People who thought they'd had a vitamin pill rated themselves as generally more invulnerable.

The Harm from Quackery

The results for smoking were more worrying. There's no doubt smoking is bad for you. There's also no doubt the motives and justifications for smoking are complex. But people who thought they'd had a vitamin pill were 50% more likely to have a cigarette—89% compared with 62%—and that result was highly statistically significant.

This might be a good moment to pause and remember that the Cochrane review on antioxidant vitamin pills—the pills that glossy magazines most like to recommend—found around 200,000 patients' worth of good randomised trial data, and overall, these pills do nothing to prolong life: if anything, it turns out, they actively increase your risk of dying.

So back to our study on risk compensation behaviour. They broadened the design in case students are somehow an exceptional case, and repeated the experiment with 80 new participants, aged 19 to 58, from the wider community: once again, the people who thought they'd had vitamin pills smoked more cigarettes, and once again they believed themselves to be more invulnerable to harm.

So they expanded the project even further, into two longer studies, broader in remit, and this time people who thought they'd had a vitamin pill were less likely to exercise and less likely to choose healthier food.

People often ask what the harm is from quackery. I don't think there needs to be one: quackery, overall, is more interesting than it is dangerous. But the message from these trials is clear. Believing, incorrectly, that you've done something healthy by taking a vitamin pill makes you more likely to take genuine, concrete, real-world risks with your health. It's a chilling thought, but ideas aren't without impact, and every time we humour a harmless myth—that vitamin pills are healthy, that some fashionable berry prevents cancer—we might be doing more harm than we think.

> "Supplementation with calcium plus vi-
> tamin D has been shown to be effective
> in reducing fractures and falls (which
> can cause fractures) in institutionalized
> older adults."

Supplements May Be Beneficial in Maintaining the Body's Calcium

Office of Dietary Supplements

*The Office of Dietary Supplements (ODS) of the National Insti-
tutes of Health is a US government project to provide information about vitamins and minerals. In the following viewpoint,
the ODS provides a fact sheet on calcium. The sheet says that
calcium is needed for health, and that higher levels are sometimes needed for postmenopausal women, people with lactose intolerance, and some other groups. The fact sheet suggests that
calcium supplements can be useful in maintaining bone health
and in some other situations. The ODS emphasizes that the best
source of calcium is food, and that supplements should be taken
in consultation with a physician.*

"Dietary Supplement Fact Sheet: Calcium," Office of Dietary Supplements, November 16, 2012.

As you read, consider the following questions:

1. For what functions does the body require calcium, according to the author?

2. What are the two main forms of calcium in supplements, and how do they differ, as described by the ODS?

3. What are the health risks of excessive calcium, in the author's opinion?

Calcium, the most abundant mineral in the body, is found in some foods, added to others, available as a dietary supplement, and present in some medicines (such as antacids). Calcium is required for vascular contraction and vasodilation [narrowing and widening of blood vessels], muscle function, nerve transmission, intracellular signaling and hormonal secretion, though less than 1% of total body calcium is needed to support these critical metabolic functions. Serum calcium [that is, calcium in the blood] is very tightly regulated and does not fluctuate with changes in dietary intakes; the body uses bone tissue as a reservoir for, and source of calcium, to maintain constant concentrations of calcium in blood, muscle, and intercellular fluids.

The remaining 99% of the body's calcium supply is stored in the bones and teeth where it supports their structure and function. Bone itself undergoes continuous remodeling, with constant resorption and deposition of calcium into new bone. The balance between bone resorption and deposition changes with age. Bone formation exceeds resorption in periods of growth in children and adolescents, whereas in early and middle adulthood both processes are relatively equal. In aging adults, particularly among postmenopausal women, bone breakdown exceeds formation, resulting in bone loss that increases the risk of osteoporosis over time.

Recommended Intakes

Intake recommendations for calcium and other nutrients are provided in the Dietary Reference Intakes (DRIs) developed by the Food and Nutrition Board (FNB) at the Institute of Medicine of the National Academies (formerly National Academy of Sciences). DRI is the general term for a set of reference values used for planning and assessing the nutrient intakes of healthy people. These values, which vary by age and gender, include:

- Recommended Dietary Allowance (RDA): average daily level of intake sufficient to meet the nutrient requirements of nearly all (97%–98%) healthy individuals.

- Adequate Intake (AI): established when evidence is insufficient to develop an RDA and is set at a level assumed to ensure nutritional adequacy.

- Estimated Average Requirement (EAR): average daily level of intake estimated to meet the requirements of 50% of healthy individuals. It is usually used to assess the adequacy of nutrient intakes in populations but not individuals.

- Tolerable Upper Intake Level (UL): maximum daily intake unlikely to cause adverse health effects.

The FNB established RDAs for the amounts of calcium required for bone health and to maintain adequate rates of calcium retention in healthy people. They are listed in [this viewpoint's sidebar] in milligrams (mg) per day.

Sources of Calcium

Food Milk, yogurt, and cheese are rich natural sources of calcium and are the major food contributors of this nutrient to people in the United States. Nondairy sources include vegetables, such as Chinese [napa] cabbage, kale, and broccoli. Spinach provides calcium, but its bioavailability is poor. Most grains do not have high amounts of calcium unless they are fortified; however, they contribute calcium to the diet because they contain small amounts of calcium and people consume them frequently. Foods fortified with calcium include many fruit juices and drinks, tofu, and cereals.

In its food guidance system, *MyPlate*, the U.S. Department of Agriculture recommends that persons aged 9 years and older eat 3 cups of foods from the milk group per day. A cup is equal to 1 cup (8 ounces) of milk, 1 cup of yogurt, 1.5 ounces of natural cheese (such as Cheddar), or 2 ounces of processed cheese (such as American).

Dietary supplements. The two main forms of calcium in supplements are carbonate and citrate. Calcium carbonate is more commonly available and is both inexpensive and convenient. Due to its dependence on stomach acid for absorption, calcium carbonate is absorbed most efficiently when taken with food, whereas calcium citrate is absorbed equally well when taken with or without food. Calcium citrate is also useful for people with achlorhydria [low stomach acid], inflammatory bowel disease, or absorption disorders. Other calcium forms in supplements or fortified foods include gluconate, lactate, and phosphate. Calcium citrate malate is a well-absorbed form of calcium found in some fortified juices.

Calcium supplements contain varying amounts of elemental calcium. For example, calcium carbonate is 40% calcium by weight, whereas calcium citrate is 21% calcium. Fortunately, elemental calcium is listed in the Supplement Facts panel, so consumers do not need to calculate the amount of calcium supplied by various forms of calcium supplements.

The percentage of calcium absorbed depends on the total amount of elemental calcium consumed at one time; as the amount increases, the percentage absorption decreases. Absorption is highest in doses [of less than] 500 mg. So, for example, one who takes 1,000 mg/day of calcium from supplements might split the dose and take 500 mg at two separate times during the day.

Some individuals who take calcium supplements might experience gastrointestinal side effects including gas, bloating, constipation, or a combination of these symptoms. Calcium carbonate appears to cause more of these side effects than calcium citrate, so consideration of the form of calcium supplement is warranted if these side effects are reported. Other strategies to alleviate symptoms include spreading out the calcium dose throughout the day and/or taking the supplement with meals.

Medicines. Because of its ability to neutralize stomach acid, calcium carbonate is found in some over-the-counter antacid products, such as Tums® and Rolaids®. Depending on its strength, each chewable pill or softchew provides 200 to 400 mg of elemental calcium. As noted above, calcium carbonate is an acceptable form of supplemental calcium, especially for individuals who have normal levels of stomach acid. . . .

Calcium Deficiency

Inadequate intakes of dietary calcium from food and supplements produce no obvious symptoms in the short term. Circulating blood levels of calcium are tightly regulated. Hypocalcemia [low blood levels of calcium] results primarily from medical problems or treatments, including renal failure, surgical removal of the stomach, and use of certain medications (such as diuretics). Symptoms of hypocalcemia include numbness and tingling in the fingers, muscle cramps, convulsions, lethargy, poor appetite, and abnormal heart rhythms. If left untreated, calcium deficiency leads to death.

Over the long term, inadequate calcium intake causes osteopenia which if untreated can lead to osteoporosis. The risk of bone fractures also increases, especially in older individuals. Calcium deficiency can also cause rickets, though [rickets] is more commonly associated with vitamin D deficiency.

Although frank calcium deficiency is uncommon, dietary intakes of the nutrient below recommended levels might have negative health consequences over the long term. The following groups are among those most likely to need extra calcium.

Calcium RDA and ULS

Recommended Dietary Allowances (RDAs) for Calcium

Age	Male	Female	Pregnant	Lactating
0–6 months*	200 mg	200 mg		
7–12 months*	260 mg	260 mg		
1–3 years	700 mg	700 mg		
4–8 years	1,000 mg	1,000 mg		
9–13 years	1,300 mg	1,300 mg		
14–18 years	1,300 mg	1,300 mg	1,300 mg	1,300 mg
19–50 years	1,000 mg	1,000 mg	1,000 mg	1,000 mg
51–70 years	1,000 mg	1,200 mg		
71+	1,200 mg	1,200 mg		

* Adequate Intake (AI)

Tolerable Upper Intake Levels (ULs) for Calcium

Age	Male	Female	Pregnant	Lactating
0–6 months	1,000 mg	1,000 mg		
7–12 months	1,500 mg	1,500 mg		
1–8 years	2,500 mg	2,500 mg		
9–18 years	3,000 mg	3,000 mg	3,000 mg	3,000 mg
19–50 years	2,500 mg	2,500 mg	2,500 mg	2,500 mg
51+	2,000 mg	2,000 mg		

TAKEN FROM: Office of Dietary Supplements, "Dietary Supplement Fact Sheet: Calcium," November 16, 2012. http://ods.od.nih.gov.

Postmenopausal women. Menopause leads to bone loss because decreases in estrogen production both increase bone resorption and decrease calcium absorption. Annual decreases in bone mass of 3%–5% per year frequently occur in the first years of menopause, but the decreases are typically less than 1% per year after age 65. Increased calcium intakes during menopause do not completely offset this bone loss. Hormone replacement therapy (HRT) with estrogen and progesterone helps increase calcium levels and prevent osteoporosis and fractures. Estrogen therapy restores postmenopausal bone remodeling to the same levels as at premenopause, leading to lower rates of bone loss, perhaps in part by increasing calcium absorption in the gut. However, because of the potential health risks associated with HRT use, several medical groups and professional societies recommend that postmenopausal women consider using medications, such as bisphosphonates, instead of HRT to prevent or treat osteoporosis. In addition, consuming adequate amounts of calcium in the diet might help slow the rate of bone loss in all women.

Amenorrheic women and the female athlete triad. Amenorrhea, the condition in which menstrual periods stop or fail to initiate in women of childbearing age, results from reduced circulating estrogen levels that, in turn, have a negative effect on calcium balance. Amenorrheic women with anorexia nervosa have decreased calcium absorption and higher urinary calcium excretion rates, as well as a lower rate of bone formation than healthy women. The "female athlete triad" refers to the combination of disordered eating, amenorrhea, and osteoporosis. Exercise-induced amenorrhea generally results in decreased bone mass. In female athletes and active women in the military, low bone-mineral density, menstrual irregularities, certain dietary patterns, and a history of prior stress fractures are associated with an increased risk of future stress fractures. Such women should be advised to consume adequate amounts of calcium and vitamin D. Supplements of these nutrients have been shown to reduce the risk of stress fractures in female Navy recruits during basic training.

Individuals with lactose intolerance or cow's milk allergy. Lactose intolerance refers to symptoms (such as bloating, flatulence, and diarrhea) that occur when one consumes more lactose, the naturally occurring sugar in milk, than the enzyme lactase produced by the small intestine can hydrolyze into its component monosaccharides, glucose and galactose. The symptoms vary, depending on the amount of lactose consumed, history of consumption of lactose-containing foods, and type of meal. Although the prevalence of lactose intolerance is difficult to discern, some reports suggest that approximately 25% of U.S. adults have a limited ability to digest lactose, including 85% of Asians, 50% of African Americans, and 10% of Caucasians.

Lactose-intolerant individuals are at risk of calcium inadequacy if they avoid dairy products. Research suggests that most people with lactose intolerance can consume up to 12 grams of lactose, such as that present in 8 ounces of milk, with minimal or no symptoms, especially if consumed with other foods; larger amounts can frequently be consumed if spread over the day and eaten with other foods. Other options to reduce symptoms include eating low-lactose dairy products including aged cheeses (such as Cheddar and Swiss), yogurt, or lactose-reduced or lactose-free milk. Some studies have examined whether it is possible to induce adaptation by consuming incremental lactose loads over a period of time, but the evidence in support of this strategy is inconsistent.

Cow's milk allergy is less common than lactose intolerance, affecting 0.6% to 0.9% of the population. People with this condition are unable to consume any products containing cow's milk proteins and are therefore at higher risk of obtaining insufficient calcium.

To ensure adequate calcium intakes, lactose-intolerant individuals and those with cow's milk allergy can choose nondairy food sources of the nutrient (such as kale, bok choy, Chinese cabbage, broccoli, collards and fortified foods) or take a calcium supplement.

Vegetarians. Vegetarians might absorb less calcium than omnivores because they consume more plant products containing oxalic and phytic acids. Lacto-ovo vegetarians (who consume eggs and dairy) and nonvegetarians have similar calcium intakes. However, vegans, who eat no animal products and ovo-vegetarians (who eat eggs but no dairy products), might not obtain sufficient calcium because of their avoidance of dairy foods. In the Oxford cohort of the European Prospective Investigation into Cancer and Nutrition, bone fracture risk was similar in meat eaters, fish eaters and vegetarians, but higher in vegans, likely due to their lower mean [average] calcium intake. It is difficult to assess the impact of vegetarian diets on calcium status because of the wide variety of eating practices and thus should be considered on a case by case basis. . . .

Bone Health and Osteoporosis

Bones increase in size and mass during periods of growth in childhood and adolescence, reaching peak bone mass around age 30. The greater the peak bone mass, the longer one can delay serious bone loss with increasing age. Everyone should therefore consume adequate amounts of calcium and vitamin D throughout childhood, adolescence, and early adulthood. When calcium intake is low or ingested calcium is poorly absorbed, bone breakdown occurs as the body uses its stored calcium to maintain normal biological functions. Bone loss also occurs as part of the normal aging process, particularly in postmenopausal women due to decreased amounts of estrogen.

Osteoporosis, a disorder characterized by porous and fragile bones, is a serious public health problem for more than 10 million U.S. adults over the age of 50, 80% of whom are women. (Another 34 million have osteopenia, or low bone mass, which precedes osteoporosis.) Many factors increase the risk of developing osteoporosis, including being female, thin, inactive, or of advanced age; smoking cigarettes; drinking excessive amounts of alcohol; and having a family history of osteoporosis.

Various bone mineral density (BMD) tests are available to measure the amount of calcium and other minerals in bones in the spine, hip, and/or forearm. The T-score from these tests compares an individual's BMD to an optimal BMD (that of a healthy 30-year old adult). A T-score of -1.0 or above indicates normal bone density, -1.0 to -2.5 indicates low bone mass (osteopenia), and lower than -2.5 indicates osteoporosis. Although osteoporosis affects individuals of all races, ethnicities, and both genders, women are at highest risk because their skeletons are smaller than those of men and because of the accelerated bone loss that accompanies menopause.

Osteoporosis is most associated with fractures of the hip, vertebrae, wrist, pelvis, ribs, and other bones. An estimated 1.5 million fractures occur each year in the United States due to osteoporosis. Supplementation with calcium plus vitamin D has been shown to be effective in reducing fractures and falls (which can cause fractures) in institutionalized older adults. However, among community-dwelling postmenopausal women with no symptoms of bone disease such as osteoporosis, daily supplementation with 1,000 mg or less of calcium and 400 IU [international units] or less of vitamin D will not help to prevent bone fractures. Among these healthy individuals, intakes of both nutrients at recommended levels are important to overall bone health as one ages, but greater amounts appear to provide no additional benefits to bone.

Regular exercise and adequate intakes of calcium and vitamin D are critical to the development and maintenance of healthy bones throughout the life cycle. Both weight-bearing exercises (such as walking, running, and activities where one's feet leave and hit the ground and work against gravity) and resistance exercises (such as calisthenics and that involve weights) support bone health.

In 1993, the U.S. Food and Drug Administration authorized a health claim related to calcium and osteoporosis for foods and supplements. In January 2010, this health claim was expanded to include vitamin D. Model health claims include the following: "Adequate calcium throughout life, as part of a well-balanced diet, may reduce the risk of osteoporosis" and "Adequate calcium and vitamin D as part of a healthful diet, along with physical activity, may reduce the risk of osteoporosis in later life".

Cancer of the Colon and Rectum

Data from observational and experimental studies on the potential role of calcium in preventing colorectal cancer, though somewhat inconsistent, are highly suggestive of a protective effect. Several studies have found that higher intakes of calcium from foods (low-fat dairy sources) and/or supplements are associated with a decreased risk of colon cancer. In a follow-up study to the Calcium Polyp Prevention Study, supplementation with calcium carbonate led to reductions in the risk of adenoma (a nonmalignant tumor) in the colon, a precursor to cancer, even as long as 5 years after the subjects stopped taking the supplement. In two large prospective epidemiological trials, men and women who consumed 700–800 mg per day of calcium had a 40%–50% lower risk of developing left-side colon cancer. But other observational studies have found the associations to be inconclusive.

In the Women's Health Initiative, a clinical trial involving 36,282 postmenopausal women, daily supplementation with 1,000 mg of calcium and 400 International Units (IU) of vitamin D_3 for 7 years produced no significant differences in the risk of invasive colorectal cancer compared to placebo. The authors of a Cochrane systematic review concluded that calcium supplementation might moderately help prevent colorectal adenomas, but there is not enough evidence to recommend routine use of calcium supplements to prevent colorectal cancer. Given the long latency period for colon cancer development, long-term studies are needed to fully understand whether calcium intakes affect colorectal cancer risk.

Cancer of the Prostate

Several epidemiological studies have found an association between high intakes of calcium, dairy foods or both and an increased risk of developing prostate cancer. However, others have found only a weak relationship, no relationship, or a negative association between calcium intake and prostate cancer risk. The authors of a meta-analysis of prospective studies concluded that high intakes of dairy products and calcium might slightly increase prostate cancer risk.

Interpretation of the available evidence is complicated by the difficulty in separating the effects of dairy products from that of calcium. But overall, results from observational studies suggest that total calcium intakes ≥1,500 mg/day or ≥2,000 mg/day may be associated with increased prostate cancer risk (particularly advanced and metastatic cancer) compared with lower amounts of calcium (500–1,000 mg/day). Additional research is needed to clarify the effects of calcium and/or dairy products on prostate cancer risk and elucidate potential biological mechanisms. . . .

Health Risks from Excessive Calcium

Excessively high levels of calcium in the blood known as hypercalcemia can cause renal [kidney] insufficiency, vascular and soft tissue calcification, hypercalciuria (high levels of calcium in the urine) and kidney stones. . . .

High calcium intake can cause constipation. It might also interfere with the absorption of iron and zinc, though this effect is not well established. High intake of calcium from supplements, but not foods, has been associated with increased risk of kidney stones. Some evidence links higher calcium intake with increased risk of prostate cancer, but this effect is not well understood, in part because it is challenging to separate the potential effect of dairy products from that of calcium. Some studies also link high calcium intake, particularly from supplements, with increased risk of cardiovascular disease.

The Tolerable Upper Intake Levels (ULs) for calcium established by the Food and Nutrition Board are listed in [the sidebar] in milligrams (mg) per day. Getting too much calcium from foods is rare; excess intakes are more likely to be caused by the use of calcium supplements. NHANES [National Health and Nutrition Examination Survey] data from 2003–2006 indicate that approximately 5% of women older than 50 years have estimated total calcium intakes (from foods and supplements) that exceed the UL by about 300–365 mg.

Interactions with Medications

Calcium supplements have the potential to interact with several types of medications. This section provides a few examples. Individuals taking these medications on a regular basis should discuss their calcium intake with their healthcare providers.

Calcium can decrease absorption of the following drugs when taken together: biphosphonates (to treat osteoporosis), the fluoroquinolone and tetracycline classes of antibiotics, levothyroxine, phenytoin (an anticonvulsant), and tiludronate disodium (to treat Paget's disease).

Thiazide-type diuretics can interact with calcium carbonate and vitamin D supplements, increasing the risks of hypercalcemia and hypercalciuria.

Both aluminum- and magnesium-containing antacids increase urinary calcium excretion. Mineral oil and stimulant laxatives decrease calcium absorption. Glucocorticoids, such as prednisone, can cause calcium depletion and eventually osteoporosis when they are used for months.

Calcium and Healthful Diets

The federal government's 2010 *Dietary Guidelines for Americans* notes that "nutrients should come primarily from foods. Foods in nutrient-dense, mostly intact forms contain not only the essential vitamins and minerals that are often contained in nutrient supplements, but also dietary fiber and other naturally occurring substances that may have positive health effects. . . . Dietary supplements. . .may be advantageous in specific situations to increase intake of a specific vitamin or mineral."

For more information about building a healthful diet, refer to the Dietary Guidelines for Americans and the U.S. Department of Agriculture's food guidance system, MyPlate.

The *Dietary Guidelines for Americans* describes a healthy diet as one that:

- Emphasizes a variety of fruits, vegetables, whole grains, and fat-free or low-fat milk and milk products. Many dairy products, such as milk, cheese, and yogurt, are rich sources of calcium. Some vegetables provide significant amounts of calcium, as do some fortified cereals and juices.

- Includes lean meats, poultry, fish, beans, eggs, and nuts. Tofu made with calcium salts is a good source of calcium (check the label), as are canned sardines and canned salmon with edible bones.

- Is low in saturated fats, trans fats, cholesterol, salt (sodium), and added sugars. Low-fat and nonfat dairy products provide amounts of calcium that are roughly similar to the amounts in their full-fat versions.

- Stays within your daily calorie needs.

| *"To tell people, 'Take calcium and vita-min D to prevent fractures as you get older,' that's not panning out anymore."*

Panel to Postmenopausal Women: Don't Take Vitamin D, Calcium

Janice Lloyd, Liz Szabo, and Nanci Hellmich

Janice Lloyd, Liz Szabo, and Nanci Hellmich are health and medical reporters for USA Today, *a national daily newspaper. In the following viewpoint, they report that a government task force has stated that it does not recommend taking calcium and vita-min D in order to prevent bone fractures or cancer, even for postmenopausal women. The task force says that there is no good, scientific evidence that calcium and vitamin D provide any benefit in protecting against fractures or cancer. The authors report that some experts still say there may be some benefit to taking the supplements for some groups. However, the task force's recommendation seriously calls into question the benefits of vita-min D and calcium supplements.*

As you read, consider the following questions:

1. How did the task force grab headlines recently, according to the authors?

2. What does Jen Sachek say, as quoted by Lloyd, Szabo, and Hellmich, are some of the limitations of the government's report?

3. As cited by the authors, what does Suzanne Steinbaum say are the two factors that have the greatest impact on health?

A government advisory panel's recommendation Tuesday [in June 2012] that healthy postmenopausal women should not take daily low doses of vitamin D and calcium to prevent bone fractures is a wakeup call to millions of Baby Boomer women that more is not always better.

Insufficient Evidence

The panel said there is insufficient evidence to evaluate larger doses, easy to overdo with chewy chocolate supplements that can seem like candy.

In its draft recommendations, the U.S. Preventive Services Task Force also said existing research is insufficient to assess the risks or benefits of taking vitamin D—with or without calcium—to prevent cancer in adults.

Some studies link higher levels of vitamin D with lower rates of colorectal cancer and reduced risks for other cancers, including breast, prostate and pancreatic cancer. These reports are mixed and therefore inconclusive, the advisory panel said.

This is the same panel that grabbed headlines recently by recommending against PSA (prostate-specific antigen) tests to screen for prostate cancer in healthy men and told women ages 50 to 74 to have a mammogram every other year, instead of annually.

This latest report adds to many conflicting messages about the benefits and risks of vitamin D and calcium supplements.

For years, experts have been touting the health benefits of these nutrients. Both calcium and vitamin D are key nutrients for bone health.

The Institute of Medicine, which provides independent advice on health, recommends that people daily get 600–800 IUs (international units) of vitamin D and 700–1,300 milligrams of calcium, depending on their age.

Many foods, such as milk and yogurt products, are rich in calcium and fortified with vitamin D. Sunlight triggers the production of vitamin D in skin and is a major source of the vitamin for many people.

Fractures and Kidney Stones

The task force's draft recommendation looked at doses up to 400 IUs (international units) of vitamin D and 1,000 milligrams of calcium for fracture prevention, and recommended against taking them, saying the nutrients slightly increase the risk for kidney stones. The authors add that there is insufficient evidence to draw conclusions about taking larger doses to prevent fractures.

Fractures are a significant health problem, the task force says; every year approximately 1.5 million fractures occur in the U.S. Nearly half of all women older than 50 will have an osteoporosis-related fracture during their lifetime.

"The science is still out for pre-menopausal women and men," with regard to low-dose supplements and fractures, says Timothy Wilt, the lead author on the panel report. "Many people take the supplements, but the science was insufficient to make recommendations for everyone."

Some health experts don't agree with the task force recommendation and say women should weigh options with their physicians based on their own ethnicity, diet and sun exposure, a major source of vitamin D.

The studies analyzed by the government panel have important limitations, says Jen Sacheck, an assistant professor

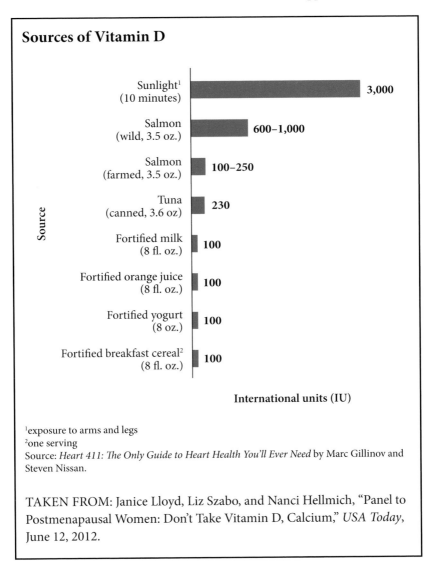

Sources of Vitamin D

Sunlight[1] (10 minutes): 3,000
Salmon (wild, 3.5 oz.): 600–1,000
Salmon (farmed, 3.5 oz.): 100–250
Tuna (canned, 3.6 oz): 230
Fortified milk (8 fl. oz.): 100
Fortified orange juice (8 fl. oz.): 100
Fortified yogurt (8 oz.): 100
Fortified breakfast cereal[2] (8 fl. oz.): 100

Source (axis)

International units (IU)

[1]exposure to arms and legs
[2]one serving
Source: *Heart 411: The Only Guide to Heart Health You'll Ever Need* by Marc Gillinov and Steven Nissan.

TAKEN FROM: Janice Lloyd, Liz Szabo, and Nanci Hellmich, "Panel to Postmenapausal Women: Don't Take Vitamin D, Calcium," *USA Today*, June 12, 2012.

and researcher in the antioxidants research laboratory at Tufts University in Boston. The research largely involved white people and no accommodation was made for how nutritional needs may vary by where a person lives, she says.

"It's a more complex picture than they're painting," she says. "If you live in New England there are many months of the year when you're not getting adequate amounts of vitamin

D from the sun. I check blood levels of young and older people and find them to be low in New England."

If you're Hispanic, Asian or black, says Sacheck, or are lactose intolerant, you might not get enough calcium from dairy products. She says being overweight or obese . . . can also compromise the levels of the nutrients.

Taylor Wallace, senior director of scientific and regulatory affairs for the Council for Responsible Nutrition, a trade group that represents supplement makers, says research shows that supplementation with calcium and vitamin D is beneficial for bone health, particularly in post-menopausal women and the elderly. "You want to try your best to get your calcium and vitamin D from food, but most Americans do not, so when there is a gap, they can fill that gap with supplements."

He points out that last month [May 2012] this same government task force said supplementation with vitamin D was beneficial in preventing incidences of falls among adults ages 65 and older. "Since falls commonly result in fractures, it's common sense for the elderly to consider supplementing with vitamin D and calcium."

About 22% of U.S. adults report taking calcium supplements and 22% report using vitamin D supplements, the industry group says.

Most calcium supplements also contain vitamin D because the two nutrients work together, Wallace says. "Vitamin D helps pull calcium into the bones."

"We recommend consumers read the labels," on supplements, he adds. "More is not always better, including for the tasty stuff like the soft chews where people might be tempted to eat a bit more."

Everything Has Changed

Suzanne Steinbaum, director of women and heart disease at Lenox Hill Hospital in New York and an American Heart Association spokeswoman, says the recommendation "changes everything. There seems to be no place for calcium for preventing cancer and fractures.

"To tell people, 'Take calcium and vitamin D to prevent fractures as you get older,' that's not panning out anymore," she says. "Even if you are at risk for a fracture, maybe you have to try other lifestyle changes, like diet and weight-bearing exercise."

Clifford Rosen, a spokesman for the Society of Bone and Mineral Research, notes that the task force discounts a finding from the Women's Health Initiative, a study of 36,282 healthy postmenopausal women, that supplements offer a 10%–11% reduced risk of fractures.

"I think the government panel's report is a little confusing," Rosen says.

JoAnn Manson, one of the Women's Health Initiative investigators, says in addition to reporting the lower fracture rate, the initiative found "bone density improved among postmenopausal women taking supplements."

Recent research has linked calcium supplements to increased risk of heart attacks, Manson says; she adds that it is best to get calcium from the diet, but some may want to add a low-dose supplement to reach recommended levels.

"The key point about calcium is that more is not better," says Manson, chief of the division of preventive medicine at Brigham and Women's Hospital in Boston.

The National Cancer Institute is funding a 20,000-person study to find whether taking a daily dietary supplement of 2,000 IU of vitamin D or one gram of omega 3 fatty acids reduces the risk of cancer, heart disease and stroke. Manson is directing the study and recruiting men and women for it through this year.

"The science is still out on cancer prevention," says Wilt.

Steinbaum acknowledges that consumers may feel confused and frustrated by changing recommendations. She hopes that people won't give up and feel there's nothing they can do to improve their health. The two old standbys—"eating better and exercising"—still have the greatest impact, she says.

> "Well-rounded, home-cooked meals aren't always possible. That's why pediatricians may recommend a daily multivitamin or mineral supplement."

Vitamins for Kids: Do Healthy Kids Need Supplements?

WebMD

WebMD is an American company that provides online health information services. In the following viewpoint, it contends that the best source of vitamins and minerals is healthy foods, especially fruits and vegetables, but that in cases where children are not getting all the nutrients they need, careful use of vitamin supplements may be helpful. The author maintains that supplements should be taken in consultation with a doctor and should not be seen as a substitute for a healthy diet.

As you read, consider the following questions:

1. Under what circumstances does the author say that pediatricians may recommend a daily multivitamin?

2. Why does WebMD say that megavitamins are a bad idea for children?

3. What does the author say that parents should do if a child will not eat a particular food?

If you believe the ads, every kid needs a daily Flintstone or Gummy Bear vitamin. But is it true?

Not necessarily so, the experts agree. Ideally, kids should get their vitamins from a balanced, healthy diet that includes:

Milk and dairy products like cheese and yogurt (preferably low-fat products for kids over age 3)

Plenty of fresh fruits and leafy, green vegetables

Protein like chicken, fish, meat, and eggs

Whole grains like steel-cut oats and brown rice

Which Kids Need Vitamin Supplements?

Given the reality of time-crunched parents, those well-rounded, home-cooked meals aren't always possible. That's why pediatricians may recommend a daily multivitamin or mineral supplement for:

Kids who aren't eating regular, well-balanced meals made from fresh, whole foods

Finicky eaters who simply aren't eating enough

Kids with chronic medical conditions such as asthma or digestive problems, especially if they're taking medications (be sure to talk with your child's doctor first before starting a supplement if your child is on medication)

Particularly active kids who play physically demanding sports

Kids eating a lot of fast foods, convenience foods, and processed foods

Kids on a vegetarian diet (they may need an iron supplement), a dairy-free diet (they may need a calcium supplement), or other restricted diet

Kids who drink a lot of carbonated sodas, which can leach vitamins and minerals from their bodies

Top Six Vitamins and Minerals for Kids

In the alphabet soup of vitamins and minerals, a few stand out as critical for growing kids.

Vitamin A promotes normal growth and development; tissue and bone repair; and healthy skin, eyes, and immune responses. Good sources include milk, cheese, eggs, and yellow-to-orange vegetables like carrots, yams, and squash.

Vitamin Bs. The family of B vitamins—B2, B3, B6, and B12—aid metabolism, energy production, and healthy circulatory and nervous systems. Good sources include meat, chicken, fish, nuts, eggs, milk, cheese, beans, and soybeans.

Vitamin C promotes healthy muscles, connective tissue, and skin. Good sources include citrus fruit, strawberries, kiwi, tomatoes, and green vegetables like broccoli.

Vitamin D promotes bone and tooth formation and helps the body absorb calcium. Good sources include milk and other fortified dairy products, egg yolks, and fish oil. The best source of vitamin D doesn't come from the diet—it's sunlight.

Calcium helps build strong bones as a child grows. Good sources include milk, cheese, yogurt, tofu, and calcium-fortified orange juice.

Iron builds muscle and is essential to healthy red blood cells. Iron deficiency is a risk in adolescence, especially for girls once they begin to menstruate. Good sources include beef and other red meats, turkey, pork, spinach, beans, and prunes.

Megavitamins—large doses of vitamins—aren't a good idea for children. The fat-soluble vitamins (vitamins A, D, E,

Vitamin A for Children

Vitamin A (and beta-carotene, which is converted into vitamin A in the body) is involved in defending the body against microbes. In countries with insufficient food supply, such as many African countries, vitamin A supplements given to children ages 6 months to 5 years lowered their risk of death by up to 30 percent. In particular, fewer children died from measles and diarrhea, both frequent causes of death in undernourished children. In contrast, vitamin A had no effect in these children on the risk of severe pneumonia, another frequent cause of childhood death. In countries with adequate food supply and nutrition, however, studies have not shown a benefit of vitamin A supplements in healthy children and adults who consume a good diet. In fact, giving high doses of vitamin A can cause serious problems. Vitamin A supplements are not necessary for children who eat a full and balanced diet.

Athena P. Kourtis,
Keeping Your Child Healthy in a Germ-Filled World, *2011.*

and K) can be toxic if kids overdose on excessive amounts. Ditto with iron. Your kids *can* get too much of a good thing.

Look to Fresh Foods for the Best Vitamins

Healthy kids get their best start from what you put in your grocery cart.

Good nutrition starts by serving a wide variety of whole, fresh foods as much as possible. That's far better than serving up fast foods or convenience foods—and hoping that taking a kids' vitamin will undo any nutritional no-no's. You'll find the most vitamins and minerals in foods high in carbohydrates and proteins (rather than fats). By far, the most high-vitamin foods of all are fresh fruits and vegetables.

To give kids more vitamins, aim for *more variety*—not simply *more food*. Twice as many kids today are overweight than just two decades ago, so use kid-sized food portions, which are one-quarter to one-third the size of adult portions.

Spread the variety of foods into several small meals and snacks throughout the day. If your child won't eat a particular food for a few days—like vegetables—don't fret. But reintroduce those foods again a day or two later, perhaps prepared in a different way. Kids' "food strikes" usually end by themselves.

Vitamins and Healthy Kids: Five Tips

1. Put vitamins away, well out of reach of children, so your child doesn't treat them like candy.

2. Try not to battle over foods with your kids or use desserts as a bribe to "clean your plate." Instead, try giving a chewable vitamin as a "treat" at the end of a meal. Fat-soluble vitamins can only be absorbed with food.

3. If your child is taking any medication, be sure to ask your child's doctor about any drug interactions with certain vitamins or minerals. Then the supplement won't boost or lower the medication dose.

4. Try a chewable vitamin if your child won't take a pill or liquid supplement.

5. Consider waiting until a child is 4 years old to start giving a multivitamin supplement unless your child's doctor suggests otherwise.

Sound nutrition plays a role in your child's learning and development. So rather than relying on cartoon characters selling supplements, commit to feeding a range of healthy foods to your kids if at all possible.

> *"In general, the data regarding the benefits of taking vitamins is weak, . . . and the data for children is pretty much nonexistent."*

Supplements for Kids: There's Not Much Evidence That They're Valuable

Gisela Angela Telis

Gisela Angela Telis has written for the Washington Post *and the* Christian Science Monitor. *In the following viewpoint, she contends that there is generally no need for children to take vitamins as a healthy diet should provide most children with all the nutrients they need. She notes that the one exception may be vitamin D, since people who are not exposed regularly to sunlight sometimes have trouble getting enough of this nutrient. However, she concludes that in most cases taking or not taking a vitamin will not make a huge difference one way or another and that children in general need fewer vitamin supplements than parents provide.*

As you read, consider the following questions:

1. Why does William Rees say that even children with less-than-ideal diets usually do not need vitamin supplements, as reported by the author?

2. Why do breast-fed babies especially need vitamin D supplements, according to Telis?

3. What are the benefits of omega-3 fatty acids, in the author's opinion?

I didn't take vitamins growing up, so when I pass the supplements aisle at the grocery store and see bottle after gleaming bottle of children's vitamins—in their enticing chewable, candy-flavored and cartoon-shaped glory—I can't help but wonder: Is this really necessary? Do kids actually need supplements?

Many parents seem to think so. After all, about half of all young children (and 30 percent of teens) have taken dietary supplements, according to a 2004 study in *Pediatric Annals*. But scientists aren't so sure.

"In general, the data regarding the benefits of taking vitamins is weak," said biochemist Thomas Sherman, a neuroendocrinologist and an associate professor at Georgetown University School of Medicine. "And the data for children is pretty much nonexistent."

What researchers do know is that most kids can get the nutrients they need from a healthful diet alone. Thanks to fortified milks, cereals and other foods, even children with less-than-ideal diets will still be okay, said William "Biff" Rees, head of the Virginia chapter of the American Academy of Pediatrics.

"I've been in practice a long time," said Rees, who has been seeing families in Fairfax County for 37 years, "and I can't remember seeing a vitamin-deficient child who didn't have some sort of illness underlying the deficiency. It's really hard to get vitamin-deficient—you almost have to work at it."

So if your child is healthy, the bottom line seems to be that you don't need to worry about a daily multivitamin or, for the most part, individual ones. Both Sherman and Rees recommend getting children the vitamins they need by focusing on food instead. Well-balanced meals with plenty of fruit and vegetables will provide kids with most of the vitamins and minerals they need for good health, along with great eating habits for the rest of their lives.

But there are a few exceptions where food alone won't do the trick. The big one is Vitamin D, which is critical for building strong bones and may protect against cancer and some other diseases. Very few foods naturally have high levels of Vitamin D. Our bodies produce most of the Vitamin D we need through exposure to sunlight—or at least they are supposed to.

Although researchers disagree over how much Vitamin D we need—the Institute of Medicine recommends 400 to 800 international units a day, but some experts call for as many as 5,000 IUs—they know that many of us don't get enough. That means kids, too: A 2008 study found about 40 percent of children have inadequate or less than optimal levels.

"We treat the sun like a death star, particularly when it comes to our kids," Sherman said. "We slather on the sunscreen, we put on hats and long sleeves and even put shades on strollers, so we're all chronically deficient in Vitamin D."

That's why many experts recommend Vitamin D supplements for kids of all ages, from babies to teens. Breast-fed babies especially should get that extra Vitamin D, because breast milk tends to have lower Vitamin D levels than fortified formulas do.

If your child has to follow a special diet or has special nutritional requirements, it may be worth considering other supplements. Kids who don't eat meat or dairy products, for example, can miss out on key nutrients. "Vegetarian kids you can raise without supplements if you're careful," said Rees. "Vegan is difficult but not impossible to do."

The risk with meat- or dairy-free diets is that your child may not be getting enough iron, calcium or B vitamins. Rees suggests working with your pediatrician to monitor your child's diet and vitamin and mineral intake, adding supplements if there are concerns.

Medical conditions (such as cystic fibrosis) that limit how well a person can absorb vitamins from food may also make supplements important. In all cases, parents should ask their pediatricians what's needed.

One supplement that's especially popular right now is omega-3 fatty acids. In a national study that used data from 2002 and 2007, 40 percent of adults who said they take supplements reported using omega-3 fatty acids—usually in the form of fish oil pills—in the past 30 days.

There's no question that omega-3s, which are found in salmon, sardines and other seafood, are important to health. They are thought to help protect heart and brain health as we age and to play a critical role in normal growth and brain development. Studies have linked omega-3s to a variety of things, including sharpened vision in infants and higher scores in reading and spelling in grade-schoolers.

So should your child take fish oil pills?

Here, again, experts recommend turning to food first. Eating fish twice a week will take care of your child's omega-3 needs, Sherman said, without need for the supplements, which even in the sweetened gummy version have a slight fishy taste and smell.

"It's cheaper to buy canned sardines or anchovies than to buy supplements, and you'll get rich, high-quality omega-3," he said. "Now, if your child doesn't eat fish or you're worried about mercury poisoning, then you can try to give your kids fish oil. But I have a hard time picturing them taking it."

For Sherman, the supplement question became the subject of discussion in his own household. In the end, he and his wife decided to give their three children Vitamin D supplements and let healthful meals do the rest. But he says he understands wanting to use supplements as insurance to make sure your kids don't miss anything they need.

"Whatever you decide, it's not a choice you should have a tremendous amount of angst about," Sherman said. "It isn't a life-or-death choice, and if it gives you one less thing to worry about, then go for it."

But he emphasized that it's important not to overdo vitamins. So whatever you decide, be sure to talk to your pediatrician before taking action.

Periodical and Internet Sources Bibliography

The following articles have been selected to supplement the diverse views presented in this chapter.

Eliseo Guallar, Saverio Stranges, Cynthia Mulrow, Lawrence J. Appel, and Edgar R. Miller III	"Enough Is Enough: Stop Wasting Money on Vitamin and Mineral Supplements," *Annals of Internal Medicine*, December 17, 2013.
Jay L. Hoecker	"Multivitamins: Do Young Children Need Them?," Mayo Clinic, n.d. www.mayoclinic .com.
Chris Kresser	"Calcium Supplements: Why You Should Think Twice," Chris Kresser, March 8, 2013. http:// chriskresser.com.
Mayo Clinic	"Calcium and Calcium Supplements: Achieving the Right Balance," September 28, 2012. www .mayoclinic.com.
Aparna Narayanan	"Study Finds Mismatch Between Kids and Vitamins," Reuters, July 6, 2012. www.reuters .com.
Alice Park	"Vitamins and Supplements Linked to Higher Death Risk in Older Women," *Time*, October 11, 2011.
Susan Shepherd	"Op-Ed: How to Start a Child Survival Epidemic," Doctors Without Borders, October 15, 2012. www.doctorswithoutborders.org.
Nancy Shute	"Most People Can Skip Calcium Supplements, Prevention Panel Says," *Shots* (blog), National Public Radio, February 25, 2013. www.npr.org.
Neil Wagner	"Are Supplements Killing You? The Problem with Vitamins, Minerals," *Atlantic Monthly*, November 16, 2011.

OPPOSING VIEWPOINTS® SERIES

CHAPTER 3

Are Weight-Loss Supplements and Athletic Supplements Beneficial?

Chapter Preface

S tarting in 2006, a workout supplement known as Jack3D (pronounced "jacked") began to get rave reviews from bodybuilders and athletes. The product was supposed to allow athletes to achieve intense focus and lift more weight faster than they ever had before. It was also supposed to be a natural substance, derived from geraniums, and completely safe when used as directed.

Soon, though, it became clear that there was more to Jack3D. The supplement's active ingredient was DMAA (1,3-dimethylamylamine), a stimulant with effects similar to amphetamines. DMAA was not natural; it was a synthetic drug. And it had dangerous side effects, including elevated heart rate, high blood pressure, nausea, cold sweats, and perhaps even addiction.

One user described his experience with Jack3D in a February 1, 2013, article in the British newspaper the *Guardian*: "I felt so pure and positive. I'd stay in the gym for hours with this laser-like focus. The only downpoint was that when I got home after exercising, I couldn't eat. It was actually hard work to get a protein shake down me. Sleeping was also a problem: I learnt not to take Jack3d less than 10 hours before I wanted to sleep."

He went on, describing how the side effects got worse, and included sudden bouts of exhaustion, and a racing heartbeat. There was one frightening incident when he had lockjaw and could not open his mouth.

For others, the effects were even worse. Michael Lee Sparling, a twenty-two-year-old US Army private in excellent physical condition, died of a heart attack after a ten-minute run following the ingestion of Jack3D. A thirty-year-old runner, Claire Squires, also took Jack3D before participating in the 2012 London Marathon. She died of heart failure a mile before the finish line.

Representatives of Jack3D denied that their supplement was responsible for the deaths. But regulators soon decided that DMAA was unsafe for use. The substance is now banned in the United States, Canada, New Zealand, Sweden, Australia, Britain, and Brazil. It is also banned by numerous sporting bodies as a performance-enhancing drug. The dangers of the substance, and the tragedies associated with it, have raised many questions about whether there needs to be tighter regulation of dietary supplements—especially of athletic supplements.

The viewpoints in this chapter offer opposing viewpoints about the effectiveness and safety of other weight-loss and athletic dietary supplements.

> *"The supplements listed here [have] positive scientific evidence supporting their use for weight loss."*

7 New Weight Loss Supplements That Really Work

Melanie Haiken

Melanie Haiken is a writer and editor whose writing has appeared in Health, Parenting, *and numerous other venues. In the following viewpoint, she asserts that a number of supplements have good scientific evidence supporting their weight-loss efficacy. To evaluate these supplements, she looked at recommendations of naturopathic doctors and at the database of the reputable organization Natural Standard. Among the supplements that she contends are effective are hydroxycitric acid (HCA), which is derived from a traditional Indian folk remedy; whey protein; and African mango seed, which is a traditional African weight-loss remedy.*

As you read, consider the following questions:

1. How does HCA contribute to weight loss, according to Haiken?

2. What is chitosan, as described by the author?

3. Besides assisting with weight loss, what therapeutic qualities does Haiken say that glucomannan has?

With all the new weight loss medications entering the market—and engendering controversy—many people are also looking to supplements to aid weight loss. But a visit to those shelves at your local Whole Foods or other health food store, and you're guaranteed to feel overwhelmed. Which really work and which don't? And are they safe?

For information, I looked at the recommendations of prominent naturopathic doctors and the organization Natural Standard, a reputable database of the latest research on supplements. You've likely never heard of many of the supplements listed here, but they've all a Natural Standard Grade A or B for having positive scientific evidence supporting their use for weight loss. . . .

HCA, Chitosan, and Whey

1. Hydroxycitrate, Hydroxycitric Acid, or HCA

HCA is actually a salt derived from the rind of dried fruit, in particular the Southeast Asian plants brindal berry and Garcinia cambogia. A traditional Indian folk remedy, HCA has been used to treat joint and stomach problems. It's sold in drug stores and supplement stores as HCA, brindleberry or brindal berry and garcinia, and is the primary ingredient in diet products with names like Citrilite, Citrin, PhyrtriMax, Bio-Max 3000, and Garcinia Trim-Pulse. Research backs the effectiveness of HCA at reducing fat absorption, increasing fat metabolism, inhibiting appetite, and lowering LDL [low-density lipoprotein, or "bad"] cholesterol.

"I'm part of a double-blind study to see how weight loss supplements help people lose weight. I'm guessing I received the sugar pill placebos."

2. Chitosan

Read about the origins of chitosan and it sounds pretty gross. Chitosan is a fiber that comes from chitin, which is the main component in the shells (or exoskeletons, for you scientific types) of insects and crustaceans. Recommended by wholistic practitioners to lower cholesterol, chitosan has also been promoted as a type of dietary fiber that may help reduce the absorption of fat.

3. Whey Protein

Health and sports supplement stores have been touting the benefits of whey protein for years, but mainly for building muscle, which it appears to do. However, whey protein also suppresses appetite, thus helping you eat less. Whey protein, which as you can guess is derived from the whey of milk, is an easily digestible form of protein. It contains high levels of the amino acid cysteine. And having more muscle helps with weight loss too.

Other Supplements

4. Beta Glucan

A concentrated soluble fiber derived from yeasts, mushrooms, and algae, beta-glucans come in many forms but all have the effect of lowering cholesterol with the additional benefits of weight loss and helping control diabetes.

5. Conjugated Linoleic Acid, or CLA

Omega 3 fatty acids and healthy fats are beneficial for all sorts of things, from brain health to heart health. But one of them, CLA, seems to aid in weight loss as well (in addition to having anticancer benefits). CLA is found primarily in beef and dairy products, so if you're vegetarian or vegan, you likely aren't getting enough. CLA-enriched daily products are in the works, but right now you have to take a supplement, most of which are derived from safflower oil. CLA is one of the more popular health food supplements for reduction of body fat, though the evidence is mixed. Animal studies have shown it to be effective, but human studies have been mixed.

6. Glucomannan

Derived from an Asian plant called Konjac, glucomannan is a fiber considered extremely effective for diabetes and blood sugar control, with the additional properties of weight loss. Glucomannan has traditionally been an important food source—whether fried, baked, or as a candy. The fiber helps absorb water in the digestive tract, reducing cholesterol and carbohydrate absorption, and research supports its role as an obesity treatment. Glucomannan is also traditionally used as a gel to be applied to the skin.

7. Mango Seed Fiber

Fiber from the seeds of the African mango tree is a traditional African weight loss remedy that's finding new popularity either alone or combined with other dietary supplements. It's most commonly used in Africa as a natural antibiotic and pain reliever. It's currently being studied for weight loss, diabetes and cholesterol reduction.

> "Regarding weight-loss supplements, . . .
> make lifestyle changes instead of pop-
> ping an ineffective, potentially danger-
> ous pill."

Weight-Loss Supplements Are Dangerous and Ineffective

Kassi Putnam

At the time of writing this article, Kassi Putnam was a graduate science student in the Department of Food Science and Human Nutrition at the University of Maine. In the following viewpoint, she argues that weight-loss supplements are insufficiently regulated and that many contain ingredients that are unsafe and potentially deadly, adding that they are ineffective as well. She contends that supplement companies make false claims and mislead the public. The best, safest way to lose weight, she concludes, is to eat well and exercise more.

As you read, consider the following questions:

1. How did the DSHEA change the regulation of weight-loss supplements, according to Putnam?

2. What is ephedra, as described by the author?

3. What percentage of men and women use dietary supplements, according to Putnam?

While standing in the checkout line at the dollar store the other day, I noticed they had the "Stacker 2" weight-loss pill for sale. The package stated in big, bold letters that it is the "world's strongest fat burner," but in the corner, in much tinier print, was the disclaimer "this statement has not been evaluated by the Food and Drug Administration [FDA], this product is not intended to diagnose, treat, cure or prevent any disease."

No Proof of Safety

We have the Dietary Supplement Health and Education Act of 1994 (DSHEA) to thank for this outrageous exaggeration, as it radically changed the regulatory framework for weight-loss supplements. Before the passage of DSHEA, the FDA's role was to provide clearance for weight-loss supplements before they went on the market. After DSHEA was passed, however, the FDA's role became one of post-market enforcement.

So what does this mean? Essentially, it indicates that companies are allowed to manufacture and market weight-loss products without consent or approval from anyone. The responsibility of ensuring that products are both safe and effective is now in the hands of industry. And furthermore, unlike prescription drug companies that are obligated to report adverse events with the use of their product, dietary supplement companies have no such regulations imposed upon them.

Do not let the term "dietary supplement" fool you. The terms "dietary" or "natural" printed on the label of a weight-loss pill do not ensure that the product is safe. You may remember the FDA's ban on the sale of dietary supplements containing ephedra in 2004. Ephedra is a "natural" product, an herb that has been used in Traditional Chinese Medicine (TCM) for thousands of years. When taken out of the TCM context and put into dietary supplements in concentrated amounts, ephedra can actually be very dangerous and potentially deadly.

Ephedra and Aurantium

Before the announcement of the FDA ban, it was estimated that approximately 2 million adults took ephedra-containing products daily, and several deaths resulted as a consequence. What did we learn from this? Sadly, not so much.

Eight of the leading manufacturers of ephedra-containing supplements now sell products containing the herb citrus aurantium, more commonly known as "bitter orange." The active ingredient in citrus aurantium extract is synephrine, which contains products that may lead to adverse cardiovascular mishaps. From 1998 to 2004, Health Canada reported 16 events in which products containing bitter orange were associated with irregular heartbeat, severely abnormal heart rhythm, sudden collapse, blackout and cardiac arrest.

Celebrity trainer Jillian Michaels of "The Biggest Loser" fame and the company Thin Care is currently being sued by three individuals who have tried its "Maximum Strength Calorie Control Pills", containing bitter orange. One lawsuit states that the supplements are made with a "potentially lethal" ingredient that can lead to high blood pressure and heart problems. Michaels still stands behind her product and Thin Care is confident that it will win the lawsuit.

Does the American public have to experience a certain number of adverse effects or multiple deaths before products such as these are regulated? Citrus arantium is not the only herb being disguised as a safe and effective treatment for weight loss, with many other supplements containing ingredients that have not been adequately tested.

People are putting themselves in danger for absolutely no valid reason. There have been numerous studies done on the efficacy of weight-loss supplements and there is little evidence that any dietary supplement on the market today is effective. The supplement industry is simply capitalizing on people's desires to lose weight through the use of false or misleading claims. This is one situation where the risks definitely outweigh the benefits.

At any given time, one-third of men and one-half of women in the United States are trying to lose weight. Roughly 21 percent of women and 10 percent of men have used some type of dietary supplement in an effort to do so. Until we are able to enforce more strict regulations regarding weight-loss supplements, do yourself a favor, and make lifestyle changes instead of popping an ineffective, potentially dangerous pill.

A healthy diet in combination with regular physical activity is the key to successful long-term weight loss and the magnitude of benefits received as a result will far outweigh the risks.

| "Supplements can act as a safeguard to make sure that [athletes] are getting the right daily values of required nutrients."

Supplements May Help Athletic Performance If Taken with Care

Davy Kestens

Davy Kestens is an Internet entrepreneur, the founder of Twitspark, and an avid runner. In the following viewpoint, he argues that dietary supplements can be helpful for runners. This is especially the case, he asserts, for runners who are not getting enough nutrients, proteins, vitamins, or minerals. Kestens says that runners need to be careful not to overdo any of these substances. He adds that other dietary supplements may not be scientifically proven to improve performance, but he contends that many runners say they have experienced benefits from such supplements.

As you read, consider the following questions:

1. What does Kestens say the body uses protein for?

2. According to the author, why may runners need iodine supplements?

3. What herbs does Kestens say that some runners take?

Runners can demand much from their bodies, so it only makes sense to put as much care back in to improve performance and to augment recovery. Whether one is a competitive runner or whether you just run to keep fit, the idea of taking supplements is one many consider.

The general types of supplements are the essential nutrients—protein, vitamins and minerals—and other types of supplements that are not considered as "required" for good health.

The latest trend is to advise against "mega-dosing" any type of supplement. In fact, according to many experts it is possible to get all the nutrition one needs from a good balanced diet. However, many runners may fail to get sufficient nutrients for a variety of reasons including dieting, poor eating habits, etc. At the very least, supplements can act as a safeguard to make sure that you are getting the right daily values of required nutrients. Some non-essential supplements may also help, and many are widely supported by successful competitive runners. However, at the same time, there may be dissenting voices as to the efficacy of these supplements in the medical community.

Protein and Muscles

The body uses protein to repair and strengthen muscles that are damaged during running and other types of strenuous physical activity.

Weight-lifters and body builders are known to concentrate on high protein diets in combination with protein supplementation usually in the form of nutritional shakes and energy bars. Runners also need strong muscles although it is mainly sprinters who require significant increases in muscle mass. For distance runners, too much muscle mass may act as a detriment.

Most athletes probably get sufficient protein from their diets especially in Western countries in which meat forms a large portion of the meal. However, some runners may not consume enough protein in food for various reasons.

Runners who do not consume enough protein can use supplements including high protein shakes. However, they should be careful not to overdo the supplementation. Even competitive runners only require slightly more protein intake. Consuming more than two grams of protein daily for each kilogram of body weight is excessive even for athletes.

Excess protein can lead to toxic conditions due to increased urea production. Too much protein might also be stored by the body as fat. Some studies have shown that excessive protein can lead to dangerously high blood ammonia concentrations and can lead to an overly acidic digestive tract.

Vitamin and Mineral Supplements

Since food today is generally fortified with vitamins and minerals, it is much easier to get the recommended daily values than before.

However, if you eat lots of natural and organic food, these often are not fortified at all. Also, if your diet is not balanced you may not get enough of the essential vitamins and minerals. For example, if you are on a low salt diet, then you could very well suffer from iodine deficiency.

Most Westerners get their iodine from iodized salt. Iodine is essential for a healthy thyroid gland. Because of the widespread growth of low salt diets to combat hypertension and other health problems, the rate of thyroid-related health problems has grown. For this reason, people on low salt diets may wish to supplement their diets with iodine.

For most runners, it may be a good idea to take a vitamin and mineral supplement that provides at least the minimum daily requirements. While athletes may require more of these nutrients, loading up on them probably does not improve performance. The extra nutrition needed can probably be acquired from a healthy diet.

Note that it is easy to overload on certain vitamins and minerals. Vitamin A, for example, is stored by the body and too much of this nutrient can cause significant health problems.

While many runners like to load up on iron to increase the supply of blood oxygen, too much iron in the system can actually be counter-productive. Some studies have shown that American men are more likely to suffer from iron toxicity rather than from iron deficiency.

Other Supplements

A wide range of non-essential supplements is taken by runners and other athletes desiring to improve their performance.

For example, glucosamine and chondroitin are popularly taken to help the body repair and replenish the cartilage and lubricants of the joints. A compound known as vanadyl sulfate is thought to increase endurance and energy.

Some runners take medicinal herbs that are believed to help with athletic performance. These can range from exotic Chinese herbs such as ginseng and gingko to those found in the spice rack, including garlic and cayenne.

The efficacy of some of these supplements, as mentioned previously, can be disputed in scientific circles. Nevertheless, there are many successful runners and others athletes that believe such supplementation lead to improved results.

Deciding on whether to take supplements to improve running performance will first involve an analysis of whether you are getting all the required vitamins, minerals and protein.

For many runners, a minimal supplement will not hurt since this poses little danger of a toxic overdose. Be careful though not to overload on vitamins and minerals that are stored in the body. Even nutrients that are not stored like Vitamin C can have a negative impact when taken in megadoses.

For many successful runners, some trial and error is necessary to find what types of supplements work for them in increasing performance.

"A growing number of athletes . . . have traced a positive doping test back to a tainted supplement."

Athletes, Stop Taking Supplements

Christie Aschwanden

Christie Aschwanden is a health columnist for the Washington Post *and a contributing editor for* Runner's World. *In the following viewpoint, she argues that the supplement industry is poorly regulated and that there is little evidence that supplements help athletes. Instead, she contends, supplements may include dangerous ingredients, or chemicals that show up in drug testing. She concludes that some athletes are fooled by supplement claims, while others may take them to cover their use of steroids or other performance-enhancing drugs.*

As you read, consider the following questions:

1. What did Jessica Hardy test positive for, and what does Aschwanden say was probably the source of the illicit substance?

2. Who is the chief author and advocate of DSHEA, and why does he support the law, according to the author?

3. According to Aschwanden, why are athletes not likely to need to supplement most nutrients?

American swimmer Jessica Hardy set two world records in 2008 and was poised to take home medals from the Olympics, but she never made it to Beijing. Instead, she was booted from the Olympic team after testing positive for clenbuterol—an asthma medication that can increase muscle growth—at the Olympic trials. Like almost every athlete who's ever tested positive for performance-enhancing drugs, Hardy insisted that she hadn't doped. For once, this doesn't appear to have been an outright fib.

Tainted Supplements

What Hardy *had* taken was something called Arginine Extreme, a nutritional supplement made by AdvoCare, a multi-level marketing outfit that describes itself as a health and wellness company and that was one of her sponsors. Though clenbuterol is not listed on the ingredients list, tests presented by Hardy's defense team showed that the Arginine Extreme supplements did, in fact, contain the drug. AdvoCare disputes the evidence and denies wrongdoing. The company was not a party to the arbitration proceeding and so did not question witnesses or present evidence. AdvoCare asserts that tests conducted on its behalf by two independent laboratories found no evidence of contamination in the supplements and that the ingredients listed on the products were the only ingredients found in them. During her arbitration hearing, Hardy convinced the World Anti-Doping Agency that she'd inadvertently ingested clenbuterol via a contaminated supplement, and she received only a one-year suspension instead of the usual two-year ban. Even so, she missed both the Olympics and the World Championships and lost an opportunity not just for medals and records, but also for sponsorship opportunities and income. (She'll get another chance this month [July 2012] when she competes in London.)

Hardy is among a growing number of athletes who have traced a positive doping test back to a tainted supplement. Swimmer Kicker Vencill and cyclists Flavia Oliveira and Scott Moninger (an acquaintance of mine) also tested positive after taking supplements, and 400-meter gold medalist LaShawn Merritt linked his positive dope test to a product called Extenz that he picked up at 7-Eleven. The problem is so prevalent that the U.S. Anti-Doping Agency (USADA) has developed an educational campaign for athletes, called Supplements 411.

Supplements are risky thanks in part to a piece of legislation passed in 1994 called the Dietary Supplements and Health Education Act. The DSHEA essentially deregulated dietary supplements, including vitamins, herbs, protein shake mixes, nutritional supplements, and other powders and pills that millions of people of all levels of athletic ability might take to improve their health. Most people assume that if a product is available on store shelves, it must be OK. But supplements are not required to be evaluated or proven safe or effective before they're sold. New rules finalized in 2007 gave the FDA [Food and Drug Administration] power to regulate the manufacturing and packaging of supplements, but the agency's ability to police supplement companies remains limited by DSHEA. Its chief author and most powerful advocate is Sen. Orrin Hatch, whose home state of Utah is home to much of the U.S. supplement industry. Hatch, who attributes his good health to the supplements he takes each day, fought a recent amendment to increase the FDA's ability to regulate the industry.

Safety Problems

FDA investigations have repeatedly found safety problems with supplements, including dangerous ingredients—everything from diet pills containing a drug previously pulled from the market due to safety concerns to body-building supplements packed with anabolic [muscle-building] steroids. These are hardly isolated cases. A 2004 study found that 18 percent of nutritional supplements purchased in the United States contained undeclared anabolic androgenic [male-hormone-enhancing] steroids. The FDA has also warned consumers about supplements laced with dangerous levels of selenium and chromium. In 2009, college baseball player Jareem Gunter told a Senate hearing that he'd ended up in the hospital with liver failure after taking a body-building supplement, and late last year [2011], the Army set up a probe to investigate whether body-building supplements containing dimethylamylamine, or DMAA, a stimulant that can narrow blood vessels and arteries, were involved in the deaths of two soldiers and liver and kidney damage in others.

In April, the FDA sent warning letters to 10 supplement makers and distributors marketing "natural" stimulants such as Hemo Rage Black, Jack3D, and Biorhythm SSIN Juice that contained DMAA, warning that DMAA did not qualify as a dietary ingredient. (Manufacturers told the *New York Times* they disagreed.) A recent *Chicago Tribune* investigation reported that the FDA has discovered manufacturing violations in nearly half of the 450 dietary supplement producers it has inspected since new rules gave the agency more oversight five years ago [in 2007].

Given these dangers, why on earth would athletes take supplements? Hardy popped the pills expecting them to help her recover after races and practices. AdvoCare's website makes at least nine claims about Arginine Extreme—it can "support nutrient delivery to muscles," "promote short-term increases in nitric oxide levels," nourish "the precursors necessary for muscle growth and recovery," "enhance strength and stamina, (especially when used with AdvoCare Muscle Fuel")," and help "maintain a healthy cardiovascular system" and an "efficient immune system."

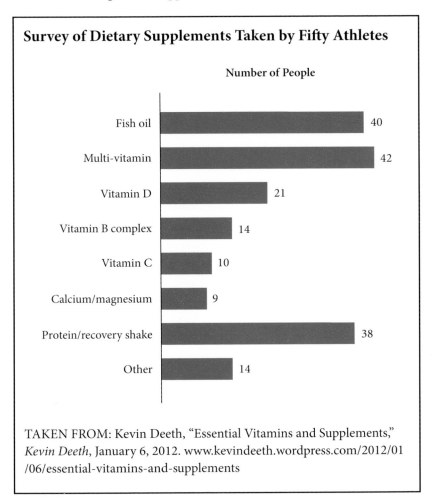

Survey of Dietary Supplements Taken by Fifty Athletes

Number of People

Supplement	Number of People
Fish oil	40
Multi-vitamin	42
Vitamin D	21
Vitamin B complex	14
Vitamin C	10
Calcium/magnesium	9
Protein/recovery shake	38
Other	14

TAKEN FROM: Kevin Deeth, "Essential Vitamins and Supplements," *Kevin Deeth*, January 6, 2012. www.kevindeeth.wordpress.com/2012/01/06/essential-vitamins-and-supplements

A Lack of Evidence

These are big promises, especially from a product whose declared ingredients consist of nothing more than some amino acids and vitamins. Like most supplements purporting to enhance athletic performance, AdvoCare's products are not backed by peer-reviewed clinical trials, just testimonials, the endorsements of professional athletes, and some scientific advisory board members with MDs or Ph.D.s behind their names. AdvoCare says that its products are subject to testing and quality assurance standards, and that in the company's history, there has been only one claim (from Hardy) that its products were contaminated.

When studies do appear to support supplement companies' claims, they are usually small and at best can offer only hints of efficacy, not definitive proof. As I learned first-hand during my earnest attempt to study the effects of beer on running, even seemingly robust study designs can lead you to a dodgy conclusion. My study could have easily been interpreted to show that beer made women better runners, but as a participant of the study, I discovered problems in the standard protocols that might not have been apparent otherwise. A series of reports published July 19 [2012] in *BMJ* [*British Medical Journal*] found "a striking lack of evidence to support claims about improved performance and recovery" made by products aimed at athletes like sports drinks and supplements and concluded that it is "virtually impossible for the public to make informed choices about the benefits and harms of advertised sports products."

Despite the scarcity of evidence, athletes continue to take supplements at high rates. A 2009 study estimated that 85 percent of elite track and field athletes took supplements, and 87 percent of Canadian athletes who participated in a survey published this year reported taking dietary supplements in the previous six months.

According to FDA rules, supplements are supposed to contain substances that could be obtained through food. That means vitamins, minerals, and nutrients like carbohydrates, amino acids, or protein. But there's no reason to think athletes benefit from supplementing their diets with these things. Elite athletes spend hours each day training and must consume thousands of calories. It's hard to become nutrient-deficient when you're eating that much. The American College of Sports Medicine's position statement says, "vitamin and mineral supplements are not needed if adequate energy to maintain body weight is consumed from a variety of foods."

Dubious Claims

The one exception is iron, which often becomes depleted in menstruating women, especially if they don't eat much meat. (Low iron stores can lead to fatigue and poor performance.) But you rarely see sport supplements touting iron. Instead, advertisements target athletes with dubious claims that supplements can boost red blood cells or build muscle "naturally." And these pitches are often shrouded in pseudo-scientific language. When a supplement is promising results that you wouldn't expect from simple good nutrition, chances are the claim is bogus or the supplement contains an illicit, undeclared drug.

The difference between winning and losing is often measured in fractions of a second, and athletes trying to bridge that gap are easy targets for quackery. After Hardy's positive test, you'd expect her teammates on the U.S. swim team to eschew supplements, but Hardy estimates that, despite her warnings, about 90 percent of the swimmers still take them.

Coaches and trainers, too, are often fooled. Most have little scientific training, and the supplement industry bombards them with literature about nutrition. And there's plenty of incentive to believe the hype. Endorsement deals from supplement companies provide a major source of income for many teams, coaches, and athletes, and trainers or coaches sometimes get paid to peddle supplements to their athletes.

Under the best-case scenario, a supplement provides an expensive source of a nutrient that the athlete could be getting from food. Worst-case scenario, it's providing dangerous levels of heavy metals, pesticide residues, undeclared drugs, or illicit performance-enhancers that may show up on a drug test. USADA provides detailed advice for athletes contemplating the use of supplements, including a list of red flags that should make them think twice about using a product, such as promises that they'll enhance muscle-building or energy or claims about "proprietary blends" that are "clinically proven."

Given the slew of high-profile doping cases traced back to supplements, and USADA's concerted efforts to educate athletes, it's hard not to suspect that some of these runners, swimmers, and cyclists know exactly what they're doing. I have no reason to think that Hardy had any intention of doping, but cases like hers may give cover to genuine cheaters. After all, the designer steroid that took down [Olympic sprinter] Marion Jones and [baseball slugger] Barry Bonds was created and distributed through a supplement company—the Bay Area Laboratory Co-operative (BALCO) that gave the scandal its name.

If I were a doper, I'd be sure to have a medicine cabinet full of supplements—ones that claim to produce the same results as my drugs. Then, if I ever tested positive for doping, I'd have a plausible excuse.

Periodical and Internet Sources Bibliography

The following articles have been selected to supplement the diverse views presented in this chapter.

Joan Salge Blake	"How to Avoid Dangerous Weight Loss and Health Fraud Scams," Boston.com, March 11, 2013. http://www.boston.com.
Huffington Post	"Weight Loss Drugs, Body Building and Sexual Enhancement Supplements Crackdown by FDA," December 15, 2010. www.huffington post.com.
Donald Kirkendall	"Knowing Your Supplements Can Help You Avoid a Positive Nandrolone Test," Active, 2013. www.active.com.
Mayo Clinic	"Over-the-Counter Weight-Loss Pills: Do They Work?," February 11, 2012. www.mayoclinic .com.
Hilary Parker	"Proven Weight Loss Supplements," WebMD, n.d. www.webmd.com.
Nationwide Children's Hospital	"Supplements: To Use, or Not to Use?," n.d. www.nationwidechildrens.org.
ScienceDaily	"Supplements Could Make Athletes Unwitting Drug Cheats," September 25, 2011. www .sciencedaily.com.
Natasha Singer and Michael S. Schmidt	"Supplements for Athletes Draw Alert from F.D.A.," *New York Times*, July 29, 2009.
Bryan Tomek	"Supplements Guide," AskMen, n.d. www .askmen.com.
US Food and Drug Administration	"Beware of Fraudulent Weight-Loss 'Dietary Supplements,'" June 16, 2012. www.fda.gov.

OPPOSING
VIEWPOINTS®
SERIES

CHAPTER 4

How Well Do Supplements Treat Different Medical Conditions?

Chapter Preface

Multiple sclerosis, or MS, is a disease in which the tissue that covers nerve cells in the brain and spinal cord becomes inflamed and is damaged. This results in a number of physical and mental symptoms, including weakness, loss of coordination, and loss of speech and vision. The disease can progress in widely variable ways; some people experience only a single attack and recover quickly, while others degenerate over time. No one is certain what causes MS, although scientists believe that it may be the result of the immune system attacking the nervous system.

Because the causes of MS are unclear, and because the progress of the disease is so different from person to person, MS "is a perfect disease for quacks," according to Dr. Stephen Barrett, writing at the website Quackwatch. With MS, he notes, it is very hard to tell whether or not a given treatment is effective, and very easy to claim that partial recovery (which is common in MS) is the result of a particular treatment.

Thus, it is not surprising that various vitamin and mineral regimens have been promoted as "cures" for MS. In most cases, there is no evidence that these treatments are effective. For example, a man named Robert Barefoot ran numerous ads claiming that his dietary supplement coral calcium had helped people with MS leave their wheelchairs and walk again. There was no evidence for this claim. The Federal Trade Commission eventually legally stopped Barefoot from running these advertisements.

Coral calcium was not a creditable cure for MS, but there has been some evidence that some dietary supplements can help reduce symptoms of the disease for some sufferers. In particular, a research paper in the September 29 *Journal of Biological Chemistry* reported on promising findings related to a substance similar to the sugar glucosamine, which is widely available as a dietary supplement many claim helps alleviate arthritis pain. Scientists found that the substance suppressed the immune system's attack on the nervous system. Lab mice with MS that were not given the supplement deteriorated and became paralyzed; lab mice that were given the supplement either got no worse or deteriorated much more slowly. Senior investigator Michael Demetriou of the University of California–Irvine, said that the study points toward the possibility of someday using dietary supplements like glucosamine to treat MS.

The viewpoints in this chapter debate the use of dietary supplements in treating specific diseases, including Lyme disease and cancer.

| "Many herbs are useful in treating common colds."

Dietary Supplements Can Help Control the Common Cold

San Francisco Natural Medicine

San Francisco Natural Medicine is a naturopathic medical clinic. In the following viewpoint the author argues that natural treatment of colds can prevent colds or shorten their duration. The viewpoint recommends the use of a number of supplements, including vitamin C and zinc. It also asserts that natural herbs can help in the treatment of colds and recommends the Chinese herbal formula known as yin chao *and Western herbs such as echinacea and goldenseal. The author stresses that herbs should be taken only according to directions.*

As you read, consider the following questions:

1. According to the author, what is the role of fever in illness?

2. What supplements and nutrients does San Francisco Natural Medicine say can be used to prevent colds?

Dr. Carl Hangee-Bauer, "The Common Cold—Natural Prevention and Treatment," San Francisco Natural Medicine, 2009. Copyright © by San Francisco Natural Medicine 2009. All rights reserved. Reprinted with permission.

3. Why does the author say that soup is beneficial in combating a cold?

Autumn typically brings San Francisco some of its nicest weather of the year. Unfortunately, it also heralds the onset of cold and flu season. Upper respiratory infections [URIs] typically begin with a sore or scratchy throat, aversion to cold or alternating chills and feverish sensations, and fatigue and muscle aches and progress to either chest symptoms, such as cough and tightness, or to sinus problems (aka "head colds"). These symptoms can last from several days to several weeks.

About the Common Cold

The common cold can be caused by a wide variety of viruses, many of which we are constantly exposed to, yet most people only "catch cold" once or twice a year. This implies that it is a decrease in our resistance, not simply exposure to a virus, which causes us to catch a common cold.

Many people take decongestants, antihistamines, cough suppressants and other over-the-counter medications to feel better and be able to continue [their] normal routines. However, these can often interfere with the body's normal defense mechanisms and can actually prolong the illness. For example, when viruses invade the lining of the respiratory tract, our tissues increase the production of mucus to "wash out" the invading organisms. This mucus is also filled with antibodies and other immune chemicals to attack these viruses. When we take antihistamines and decongestants, we put the brakes on this process, which allows the viruses to stay in the body longer.

Another example is the role of fever in illness. Many people consider fever an unpleasant symptom of disease which when overcome signals recovery from the illness. They will, therefore, take medications to reduce their fever. While it may be important to bring fevers down when they get too high, the low grade fevers (100°–102°) we get with most upper respiratory infections are actually the body's response to infection and part of the body's defense mechanisms.

Increased temperature and metabolic rate makes the immune system work more quickly and efficiently and inhibits viral reproduction. In other words, our fever isn't caused by the virus but by our immune response to the virus. Many traditional therapies for upper respiratory infections actually involve sweating or warming the body to create brief artificial fevers so our immune systems can obtain the upper hand in the battle between virus and human.

So, what can we do to prevent upper respiratory infections or deal with them effectively once we've caught a common cold? Fortunately, there are many common sense natural therapies at our disposal.

How to Prevent a Cold or Flu

The first step is prevention. Maintaining a healthy immune system is a prime way to protect against getting an excessive number of colds. Good nutrition is fundamental, with beta-carotenes (found in vegetables and fruits), vitamin C and zinc being particularly important. All of these are antioxidants which protect against free radical damage to cells and enhance a variety of immune functions.

Proper stress management is also important, as chronic stress can weaken the immune system and set us up for recurrent URIs or prolonged illness. During the stress response, chemicals are released from the adrenal glands which cause the thymus to shrink and reduce its activity. People who are under excessive stress should be certain to eat a proper diet and even supplement some of the nutrients listed above to insure good immune function.

Use of tobacco or excessive amounts of alcohol, high glucose or cholesterol levels in the blood, excessive sugar consumption and allergies have all been shown to significantly weaken the immune system. Therefore, these should be properly managed to optimize immune function.

What to Do for a Common Cold

If your efforts at prevention fail and you catch a common cold, there are many things you can do to speed your recovery. With a healthy, functioning immune system, a cold should not last more than several days. However, once a cold has taken hold, it is difficult to throw it off completely after only a few days. Do not expect immediate symptomatic results when using natural substances, as most of these assist the body in overcoming the illness as opposed to suppressing the symptoms; in fact, your symptoms may temporarily worsen, though the course of the illness is generally much shorter.

Sleep and Rest. One of my teachers at naturopathic college was fond of saying, "A cold is your body's way of telling you to take a break." We think of common colds as being minor illnesses and often try to ignore them and go on about our daily routines; this often drags out the symptoms and prolongs the illness. The importance of adequate sleep and rest cannot be overemphasized; often a day or two of bed rest can greatly shorten the severity and duration of a cold. Numerous studies have shown that potent immune activators are released and many immune functions are greatly increased during deep sleep.

Liquids. Dehydration of the respiratory tract has been shown to produce a much more hospitable environment to viruses than a moist environment. Drinking plenty of liquids helps prevent this dehydration and also improves white blood cell function. The type of liquid you drink is important; concentrated sugars such as soft drinks or fruit juices greatly reduce the ability of the white blood cells to kill bacteria and viruses.

Nutrition. Vitamin C is the most commonly mentioned vitamin in helping prevent or treat the common cold. It has

---

Vitamin C in Selected Foods

Food, Standard Amount	Vitamin C (mg)	Calories
Grapefruit juice, ¾ cup	50–70	71–86
Guava, raw, ½ cup	188	56
Red sweet pepper, raw, ½ cup	142	20
Red sweet pepper cooked, ½ cup	116	19
Kiwi fruit, 1 medium	70	62
Orange, raw, 1 medium	70	62
Orange juice, ¾ cup	61–93	79–84
Green pepper, sweet, raw, ½ cup	60	15
Green pepper, sweet, cooked, ½ cup	51	19
Mango, ½ cup	23	54
Vegetable juice cocktail, ¾ cup	50	34
Strawberries, raw, ½ cup	49	27
Brussel sprouts, cooked, ½ cup	48	28
Canteloupe, ¼ medium	47	51
Papaya, raw, ¼ medium	47	30
Kohlrabi, cooked, ½ cup	45	24
Broccoli, raw, ½ cup	39	15
Edible pod peas, cooked, ½ cup	38	34
Broccoli, cooked, ½ cup	37	26
Sweet potato, canned, ½ cup	34	116
Tomato juice, ¾ cup	33	31
Cauliflower, cooked, ½ cup	28	17
Pineapple, raw, ½ cup	28	37
Kale, cooked, ½ cup	27	18

TAKEN FROM: Mountaintop Accupuncture, "Prevent Colds with Vitamin C," November 2010.

---

been shown to be antibacterial and antiviral, though its main effect appears to be improvement in host resistance by stimulating white blood cells, increasing interferon levels and antibody response, to name a few. I typically recommend 500–1000 mg every two hours for adults during a cold.

Zinc is important. A recent double-blind clinical trial showed that using zinc lozenges in the early stages of a common cold decreased its average duration by seven days. 86% of the zinc-treated patients were completely over their colds within seven days.

Soups are excellent foods to emphasize during a cold, especially Chinese hot and sour soup. Soups provide water, are easily digested, are high in nutrients, and hot and sour soup in particular makes you sweat. (Be sure to avoid cold drafts after eating this soup). Chicken soup has also been shown to be an effective cold remedy. It contains cysteine, an amino acid which thins the mucus in the lungs, and has been shown in studies to increase air flow through the respiratory passages. Adding garlic, onions, red pepper or hot spices to your chicken soup adds to its effectiveness.

Herbs

Many herbs are useful in treating common colds, usually due to their immune enhancing effects. In Chinese Medicine, a formula called Yin Chao is often used to prevent and treat colds. If used early enough, it is often successful in stopping the cold in its early stages. This formula is widely available at herb stores in Chinatown.

In western herbal medicine, echinacea, goldenseal, and licorice are a few of the most commonly used herbs. These are all potent herbal enhancers of immune function, and when used properly, often shorten the length and severity of the average cold. These are also available in a variety of combinations at your local health food store.

Be sure to use herbs wisely and according to directions. Though these herbs are appropriate for short-term administration, long term use may decrease their effectiveness and may even cause health problems in some people.

Finally, if your common cold symptoms are particularly severe, long-lasting, or produce unusual symptoms such as extreme fatigue, painful cough, etc, be sure to contact your health care provider for an examination and appropriate treatment. Self care can be effective for most common colds, but occasionally in complicated cases professional care is necessary.

| "*Valerian could help ease some of the sleep problems that can come with menopause.*"

Valerian May Aid Menopausal Sleep Problems: Study

Amy Norton

Amy Norton is a reporter for Reuters, a major newswire. In the following viewpoint, she presents an Iranian study that found that postmenopausal women got relief from insomnia by taking capsules of the herb valerian. The study also showed few harmful side effects, indicating that taking valerian should be safe and effective. Norton notes, however, that other studies with valerian have been inconclusive, and there have been few studies of the effects of taking valerian long term. Norton also warns that valerian is not always well-regulated and that some capsules contain less valerian than advertised on the package.

As you read, consider the following questions:

1. What type of clinical trial is considered the gold standard of medical evidence, according to Norton?

2. What side effects does the author say are sometimes associated with valerian use?

3. What other treatments besides valerian does Norton say studies have found to be effective in fighting insomnia?

The popular herbal sleep aid valerian could help ease some of the sleep problems that can come with menopause, a small study suggests.

Valerian root has been used since ancient Greek and Roman times for various health problems, including insomnia. Modern science is split on whether the herb works: some studies have indicated that it can ease insomnia, but few rigorous clinical trials have put valerian to the test.

For the new study, researchers in Iran randomly assigned 100 postmenopausal women with insomnia to take either two valerian capsules or inactive placebo capsules every day for a month.

That type of clinical trial—in which neither researchers nor participants know who is taking the real treatment or the placebo—is considered the "gold standard" of medical evidence.

Overall, the study found, 30 percent of the women assigned to valerian reported an improvement in their sleep quality—which includes factors like how long it takes to fall asleep at night and how often a person wakes up overnight.

In contrast, only four percent of women taking the placebo reported better sleep.

Simin Taavoni and colleagues at Tehran University report the findings in the journal *Menopause*.

Sleep problems tend to become more common as people age, with studies suggesting that about half of older adults have insomnia symptoms, such as trouble falling asleep or staying asleep.

For women, menopausal hot flashes and night sweats can add to sleep problems.

Different Types of Insomnia

The first thing that may pop into your head when you hear the term "insomnia" is the inability to fall asleep, but the disorder manifests in many different ways as well. Though there are several different subcategories of insomnia, there are three main ways that it may affect you. Other manifestations of insomnia include having difficulty staying asleep once you doze off, or sleeping for a few hours and then waking up way too early.

For some, lack of sleep is a lifelong condition, but for others it's just a temporary condition brought on by illness or circumstance. The length of time you suffer from insomnia is largely dependent on what causes it, and the treatment plan will be based on the type that you have.

Transient Insomnia: This is by far the most common form of insomnia and will affect nearly everyone at some point. Transient insomnia is caused by temporary life circumstances, such as short-term illness, stress, travel, or other environmental or physical factors.

Chronic Insomnia: This type of insomnia is the one that really wreaks havoc on all areas of your life. It's generally caused by long-term physical or psychological issues and is extremely difficult (though not impossible) to treat.

John Chatham,
Insomnia: A Guide to Insomnia and
Relief for a Better Night's Sleep, *2012.*

The current findings are "encouraging," according to Dr. Jerome Sarris of the University of Melbourne in Australia, who was not involved in the study but has researched herbal approaches to treating insomnia, anxiety and depression.

No Harm in Trying It

And for women with sleep problems who are interested in valerian, "there is no harm in trying it," Sarris told Reuters Health in an email.

Women in this study reported no side effects, according to Taavoni's team. And in general studies suggest that any side effects from the herb are mild, like headache or upset stomach.

Valerian is also fairly cheap, with 100 capsules generally costing less than $10.

On the other hand, there's no research on the safety of long-term use, according to the U.S. National Center for Complementary and Alternative Medicine.

And despite the positive findings in the current study, there are still questions about valerian's effectiveness. In a recent review of clinical trials on alternative remedies for insomnia, Sarris and his colleagues found only weak evidence that valerian—or other herbs—work.

There was better evidence in support of yoga, tai chi and acupressure.

Lifestyle changes like cutting down on caffeine and getting regular exercise (but not too close to bedtime) are often recommended for insomnia. When those don't work, the mainstream medical fixes include prescription medications and cognitive behavioral therapy.

According to Sarris, future studies should look at valerian's effects on other measures of sleep—like the total amount of time that people taking the herb are able to stay asleep and their daytime functioning.

Women in the current study took two valerian capsules a day, each containing 530 milligrams of valerian root extract. Both the valerian and placebo capsules they used were made specifically for the study.

One question that arises when taking valerian is whether you are actually getting the amount listed on the product label.

A recent report by ConsumerLab.com, an independent testing company, found that of nine valerian supplements sold in the U.S., five had lower amounts of the herb than indicated on the packaging. That included one product with no valerian in it at all.

In the U.S., valerian and other medicinal herbs are considered dietary supplements, and not regulated in the same way as drugs.

▌ *"Valerian is ineffective at treating in-*
▌ *somnia."*

Valerian Is an Ineffective Cure for Insomnia

Examine.com

Examine.com is an online compendium on supplementation and nutrition that gathers and reports on primary research. In the following viewpoint, the site reports on studies of the herb valerian. The author concludes that there is not enough evidence to evaluate valerian's usefulness in the treatment of anxiety. The author contends that the balance of evidence indicates that valerian provides little benefit in combating insomnia but has few dangerous side effects.

As you read, consider the following questions:

1. According to the author, what did the 2010 meta-study of valerian root conclude about its treatment of insomnia?

2. What did the systematic reviews published since the meta-analysis conclude about valerian as a sleep aid, according to Examine.com?

3. What side effects does the author say result from taking valerian?

Valerian exerts most of its effects via binding to GABA [gamma aminobutyric acid] (A) receptors in the brain via its constituent valerenic acid. Its effects in this manner seem to be dose dependent.

Valerian seems to act partially as an agonist [activator] to the GABA receptor and partially as a positive modulator of the GABA(A) receptor. Potentially, this could mean synergism with Valerian and any GABA(A) agonist, including GABA itself.

There may also be interactions with the adenosine system of the brain, as evidenced by superloading valerian for use as an anti-convulsant in rats (which was partially negated with introduction of an adenosine antagonist).

Anxiety, Sleep, and Insomnia

Valerian root has traditionally been used to treat anxiety, and may act as an axiolytic [anxiety inhibitor] via its constituent valerenic acid and the GABA(A)-ergic system of the brain. Although promising, evidence is not overly available for the efficacy of valerian in treatment of anxiety disorders however.

A 2010 meta-study concluded that Valerian root was barely effective for *subjective* treatment of insomnia relative to placebo [nonactive sugar pill] and concluded that there was a lack of empircal measures in the literature and current empirical measure were limited and fairly weak in positive effect. It makes note of past reviews that, accordingly, do not include a meta-analysis, yet a systemic review suggests that Valerian is ineffective at treating insomnia (when assessing rigorous clinical interventions), one that notes a statistically significant improvement in subjective sleep-quality . . . and a third systemic review (second meta-analysis) that concludes that the literature (as of 2000) was too inconclusive and inconsistent to draw conclusions via meta-analysis. The aforementioned meta-analysis compiled studies in the latter three as well as three more trials, two standard randomized trials and a novel web-based trial with a cumulative sample of 480 persons concluded that, out of all 18 included studies (42 total assessed) that were 'quality' that met inclusion criteria noted that the mean reduction in sleep latency . . . [suggested] a poor and inconsistent reduction in time to fall asleep. Sleep quality tended to not be significantly affected, with a negative trend persisting . . . suggesting that beneficial improvements in sleep quality remain minor; the only benefit in this study was dichotomous, when 'improvement of sleep' was not measured empirically but assessed by a 'Yes' or 'No' question. No significant publication bias was noted with the 42 studies, and [it was] noted that among these studies 40% showed minimal statistical rigor.

The aforementioned meta-analysis noted that benefit tended to be found mostly in older studies, which is also where the included studies on wholly healthy persons were included. It was noted that these studies failed to mention the aromatic nature of Valerian, and thus their blinding procedures may have been subpar [that is, participants may have been able to smell the presence of valerian in their capsule].

Since publication of this meta-analysis, two more systemic reviews have been conducted on the topic of sleep aids and these do not overturn the relative lack of effect of Valerian.

Results on Valerian and Insomnia are somewhat mixed, but most recent and best evidence either suggests that Valerian is low in potency or not significantly different than placebo.

Side Effects

One study reported that the most common side effect (16% of a sample of 19) was 'vivid dreams' induced by 600mg Valerian extract.

The most commonly reported side effects of Valerian supplementation are gastrointestinal (nausea, diarrhea, pyrosis [heartburn], epigastralgia [stomach distress]) and neurological (headaches, nervousness, drowsiness), although only diarrhea differed from placebo.

> *"When fighting an autoimmune disease, it is important to arm your body with the necessary tools so . . . I took multiple [supplements] with every meal."*

How I Healed from Lyme Disease Naturally

Lindsay Wrinn

Lindsay Wrinn is an undergraduate at Fairfield University in Iowa who contracted Lyme disease (caused by a tick's bite) while she was in high school. In the following viewpoint, she asserts that antibiotics failed to cure her Lyme disease despite the promises of her doctor. She therefore turned to natural healing and dietary therapies, changed her diet, got lots of rest, and took a number of vitamins and other supplements. She contends that the supplements and other measures helped her body to begin overcoming the Lyme disease. She encourages sufferers who do not benefit from antibiotics to try the measures she did.

As you read, consider the following questions:

1. When Wrinn did not get better, what did her doctors suggest must be wrong with her?

Lindsay Wrinn, "How I Healed From Lyme Disease Naturally" first appeared in Mind BodyGreen.com, December 3, 2012. Copyright © by MindBodyGreen 2012. Reproduced with permission. All rights reserved.

2. Which vitamins does the author say she took for her Lyme disease?

3. Why does Wrinn say that Lyme disease is political?

I was diagnosed with Lyme disease in 2006, when I was a freshman in high school. I had all of the symptoms—achy joints, intense fatigue, and bouts of memory loss and severe headaches. I spent about three months on antibiotics, even though my doctors promised that the Lyme would clear up after two weeks on the bright blue pills.

Instead, I got worse and my doctors became suspicious. Finally, they suggested that my symptoms were psychosomatic and that I needed a psychiatrist, not an MD.

Frustrated and feeling hopeless, I decided to speak with a natural health practitioner. After I began taking vitamins, switched to a mostly plant-based diet, and eliminated most toxins from my environment, I felt better than I had in a long time. Eventually, I began to heal.

Here are some steps I took to heal from Lyme disease.

1. Cut down on dairy, red meat, sugar, and caffeine.

I know—ouch. The key here is moderation. The bacteria that carry Lyme, spirochetes, feed off of sugar. As a result, I had to completely forgo desserts and minimize my intake of fruits. I stopped eating red meat unless it was organic and grass-fed, and even then only once in a while. Instead of drinking pasteurized supermarket milk, I switched to raw milk from local dairy farms. I also cut out coffee and drank more herbal, healing teas. Without excess sugar and toxic chemicals, the spirochetes didn't have fuel and died off more easily.

2. I made friends with the mesclun mix.

When I first met with my nutritionist and created a plan to attack the Lyme, he gave me one order: "Eat an organic green salad every day."

And so every afternoon, I ate a huge bowl of organic baby greens with sliced carrots and cucumbers, drizzled in olive oil.

I was feeding my body with great fuel right during the time of day when my fatigue reached an all-time high. Remember, food is medicine. Feed your body with only the best, the cleanest, and the most nutritious food so that your body can do what it was meant to do: fight disease naturally.

3. I reduced foods that cause inflammation.

This includes gluten and dairy products. With the exception of raw, local milk, I avoided all dairy. A major symptom of Lyme disease is achy limbs and joints, which trace back to inflammation. (Sidenote: to help with inflamed joints, turn to some herbal therapy).

4. I started taking vitamins.

When fighting an autoimmune disease, it is important to arm your body with the necessary tools so that your system is ready for battle. I took multiple with every meal, all Standard Process brand, including cat's claw, vitamins C and B, venus flytrap, and many others. Both cat's claw and venus flytrap, specifically, do wonders for chronic diseases. If you have difficulty falling asleep, your melatonin levels might be low. Take a melatonin supplement so that your body can get all the rest it needs at night. (Of course, always check with your doctor or natural health practitioner before taking anything new).

Speaking of rest: This is not the time for taking up a new spin class or PTA responsibility.

5. I was compassionate toward my body.

Healing takes time and energy that your body may lack if it is too "busy." Instead of a vigorous Vinyasa practice, switch out a few morning routines with Yin Yoga. Go to sleep an hour earlier than you normally do. Soak in a lavender-infused bath. Turn off all electronics at 7 pm. Do not be afraid of saying no to events, meetings, and favors asked of you. This is the only body you have—treat it well, and it will return the favor.

Lyme disease is a very political illness, mostly because of the battle between the Infectious Disease Society of America

The Problem with Lyme Disease

Why diagnosis and treatment for Lyme disease are so much more contentious than for other diseases is not clear. I suspect that one key reason is that the causative agent—the spirochete bacterium *Borrelia burgdorferi*—is a uniquely complicated pathogen that presents unusually difficult challenges. If we knew which patients were actually infected and for how long, then at least some of the controversy would disappear. But the diagnostic tests are relatively poor and behave in frustrating ways—both positive and negative test results can be wrong. This leads to the misidentification of people with Lyme disease as uninfected and of uninfected people as having Lyme disease. Poor diagnostic accuracy for Lyme disease contrasts starkly with those of most other infectious diseases we commonly experience. And the consequences of misdiagnosis are often more critical for Lyme disease than for other diseases. This is because, in contrast to many other infections, our immune systems are shockingly poor at curing us of Lyme disease, leading to potentially severe disease if antibiotics are not used. On the other hand, overuse of antibiotics in patients not needing them can be strongly detrimental to the patient and can also increase the evolution of antibiotic resistance by various microbes. The lack of reliable diagnostic tests, combined with the lack of a vaccine, means that health care providers are unusually impotent in protecting and curing [Lyme] patients, and much of the health care burden shifts to patients and potential patients. The controversy itself seems to further increase the feelings of isolation and self-responsibility among patients.

Richard S. Ostfeld, Lyme Disease:
The Ecology of a Complex System, *2010.*

and Lyme patients who still have the disease after 20 years (making it chronic, which the IDSA says is impossible). There is a slew of criticism over the relationship between the IDSA and medical companies who create the antibiotics.

As a result, more and more patients are finding relief through the natural route. If you have been diagnosed with Lyme disease, or suspect that you have Lyme (the tests are 'reliably inaccurate'), you should make an informed decision for your own health.

Some family members caught the disease early and, after taking antibiotics for two weeks, felt completely fine. However, a substantial number of Lyme disease patients are not so fortunate.

Before you take an herbal or medicinal supplement, or drastically alter your lifestyle, consult with a doctor or natural health practitioner. Find what method works for you and do not be afraid to try it (even if this means taking antibiotics while following the steps outlined above.)

Stay positive and focused on healing, and it will come. In the meantime, arm your body with the fuel it needs to rebuild.

> "There is growing anecdotal evidence
> that vitamin C and perhaps some other
> mega nutritional therapies are either
> inhibiting the healing process, increas-
> ing symptoms or, even worse, exacer-
> bating the infection."

Vitamin Supplements Can Harm Those Who Suffer from Lyme Disease

Tom Grier

Tom Grier is a Lyme disease sufferer who writes for the website LymeNetEurope. In the following viewpoint, he contends that he has seen a number of cases in which vitamin C supplements appear to cause a worsening of Lyme disease. He says there are several possible reasons for this, including alterations in blood acidity. More tests are needed, he argues, to determine whether vitamin C does in fact cause a worsening of Lyme disease. In the meantime, he asserts, patients should be very cautious about using vitamin C to treat the condition.

As you read, consider the following questions:

1. According to Grier, what was Richard first diagnosed
   with, and how did he try to treat his condition?

2. How does vitamin C affect collagen, and what effect does Grier say this might have on Lyme disease?

3. How did zinc affect patients with AIDS, according to the author?

When patients get sick and stay sick, out of desperation they may turn to a variety of other treatments. With virtually no peer review medical studies to verify the effectiveness of home remedies against Lyme disease, patients are left with mostly anecdotal accounts and personal testimonies of what works and what doesn't.

I would like to submit a caution about the overuse of one such home supplement that I think may exacerbate neurological symptoms of Lyme disease. I am concerned about what I have observed in patients from two northern Minnesota Lyme disease support groups who used mega-doses of vitamin C to treat their Lyme disease.

Let me first give you a brief account of three patients who were big believers in using vitamin C to "boost" their immune systems:

Patient 1: Richard

Richard was a 38-year-old male, a special-ed teacher, who all of his life was fastidious in his diet and exercise regimen. He was what you might call a health-nut. Every day, he would exercise in the morning, then fix himself herbal teas and take an entire regimen of vitamin and herbal supplements. He adhered to a very strict macro-biotic diet. He favored eating whole grains and home-grown sprouts and juiced his own fruits and vegetables. He also took mega-doses of vitamin-C several times a day.

When Richard began experiencing loss of coordination, extreme muscle fatigue, muscle twitches, memory loss, night sweats and slurred speech, he was tentatively diagnosed with Amyotrophic Lateral Sclerosis (ALS, or Lou Gehrig's disease.)

His immediate response was to turn to natural healing methods. He increased his endeavors to boost his immune system through use of several nutritional and herbal products. Most prominently, he used Echinacea and vitamin C. He went from two grams of vitamin C a day to four grams. His neurological symptoms not only continued to advance, but his symptoms now started advancing at an alarmingly fast rate. (We have also observed that, in some Lyme patients, using Echinacea can exacerbate arthritis.)

About this time, he tested positive for Lyme disease on the ELISA [enzyme-linked immunosorbent assay] and two Western Blot tests. Richard was started on a very inadequate dosage of amoxicillin (250 mgs three times a day), and was then more or less abandoned by his family physician after three weeks of treatment. He was told by the apprehensive physician that what was left was ALS and not Lyme disease. Richard responded to this by increasing his vitamin C to six grams a day.

His family and friends were aware of Richard's disciplined home remedy self-treatment efforts, but, despite their pleas, he did not cut back. In fact, he seemed to become more resolved than ever to try to blast his condition with supplements and an organic diet.

After seeing a neurological specialist who was well versed in Lyme disease, Richard was placed on a stronger antibiotic combination regimen. To Richard, this was like poison to the body. Reluctantly and belligerently, he tried the new drug regimen. Without informing his doctor, he did what he felt was the best thing to detoxify the antibiotics: he increased his vitamin C to nine grams a day. He did not tell his treating physician about his exuberant use of home therapies, nor did he voice his strong apprehension about taking high-dose, long-term antibiotics.

His physician in Duluth [Minnesota] was reluctant to follow the heavy antibiotic regimen that Richard's out-of-state neurologist had suggested. For the next year, his family physician put Richard through an "on again, off again" regimen of treating. He would treat with three weeks, then say, "Let's wait and see what happens when we go off for awhile". Richard's health declined rapidly. His speech was now indiscernible and his mobility was greatly impaired. His mother had to force him to stop driving.

Richard now wandered aimlessly around his apartment in his stocking feet or sandals, which were often soaking wet from water spilled on his kitchen floor. His feet were severely infected with athlete's foot disease. Despite a noticeably rapid decline in his health, Richard seemed incapable and unwilling to break his routine.

Richard was reluctant to concede that his supplements and dietary life style were failing him. He continued trying to enhance traditional medicines by adding his own supplement combinations. Richard was now mixing bulk vitamin C powder in juice and drinking eleven grams a day. Ever more rapidly, he became severely impaired in his speech, his memory, his judgment and his motor skills.

A little over one year from having positive serology for Lyme, he was completely incapacitated by his disease. He was resolute to the end that his macro nutrition diet, followed by fasts and vitamin supplementation, were the answer to his health problems.

Did vitamin C contribute to Richard's extremely rapid decline and worsening of symptoms? There is no way to know for sure, but two other cases had similar scenarios.

Patient Two: Anonymous

This patient was a well educated man who, after reading books such as "Life Extension" and "Super Nutrition", was convinced that mega-doses of vitamins were not only beneficial to maintaining good health, but could help heal most sicknesses. He often talked about the role vitamin C played in building collagen and connective tissue and repairing the body. He was a big advocate, not only [of] taking large daily doses of vitamin C, but also [of] taking a non-naturally occurring fat soluble form of the vitamin called ascorbyl palmitate (vitamin C attached to a fat molecule to make it more fat soluble in order to penetrate deeper into tissue and the brain).

At age 26, this former marathon runner started taking vitamin supplements. He started with a common dosage of 500 mgs vitamin C, 400 IU vitamin E and a high-potency multivitamin. By age 30, he started having shooting chest pains, arrhythmias, depression, extreme fatigue and malaise. His natural reaction was to increase his vitamin C intake to one gram a day.

Six years later, the patient had profound exhaustion, memory problems, worsening depression and more heart arrhythmias. He now started taking two grams of vitamin C a day and added 200 mgs of ascorbyl palmitate as well as other powerful antioxidants, including BHT, BHA, and selenium. These food preservatives were touted in the book "Life Extension" as having an anti-aging effect. His condition now worsened rapidly.

Over the next six months, this patient went from being functional and employed to a man barely able to lift his head off his pillow without blacking out. He had been tested for many possible disorders, including multiple sclerosis, before it was determined—almost by accident—that he had Lyme encephalitis.

He continued taking vitamin C and other supplements throughout his first three months of antibiotics. After failing to improve, he discontinued all supplements—and promptly started to respond to antibiotics. It took another six months of antibiotics before the pressure in his head finally disappeared. He still suffers from extreme exhaustion, atrial fibrillation [heart rhythm problem], depression and lingering memory problems, but all of his symptoms have dramatically improved. He no longer takes vitamin C supplements, but does take a multi-vitamin and eats citrus fruits every day.

Patient Three: Bill

Bill was first diagnosed with neurological Lyme disease at age 55. He was always very active and in tip-top shape. Bill was a mail carrier and lean and trim from years of walking his route. Part of his daily regimen was to lift weights and take a handful of supplements, including a half gram or more of vitamin C.

Always an innately happy person, it was out of character for Bill to suddenly break down and weep or sulk in depression for weeks at a time. When he started forgetting people's names and where he lived, it was clear that there was something wrong with Bill other than simple depression.

Finally, Bill was diagnosed with late stage neurological Lyme disease and was started on 28 days of Rocephin. His recovery was remarkable. In about six weeks, he was close to his old self. He resumed his daily regimen of lifting weights and taking vitamin C. Shortly after discontinuing IV [intravenous] Rocephin, however, Bill started to decline again. Once again disoriented, he would put canned goods in the refrigerator or wander the neighborhood aimlessly, only half-dressed in the winter cold.

His doctor started him on doxycycline (100 mg BID [twice daily]), but it did nothing to abate his worsening symptoms. Because he failed to respond, it was assumed that what he had was not Lyme disease. At the urging of his wife, Bill tried several more antibiotic regimens. Nothing seemed to have the same immediate and dramatic effect of Rocephin. After a year of this yo-yo approach to therapy, his doctor told him there would be no more antibiotics. Bill was left with no alternative but to try natural methods. He continued his sit-ups, walking—and vitamin C.

Another year went by. It was obvious to all that Bill was worse than he had ever been. Although he smiled a lot and quietly acknowledged people politely, he was in constant pain and was easily confused and frustrated by the simplest of things. He often got lost if left by himself. His wife had to arrange for both a house sitter and an attendant because Bill was unsafe at home alone. When Bill became paranoid and angry towards the strangers in his house, his wife had no choice but to place him in a nursing home.

Years later, Bill is now bedridden, sedated, unable to recognize most people and still taking 500 mgs of vitamin C a day. His only truly lucid time since his diagnosis was when his in-home IV specialists requested that he not take any supplements during his therapy that were not ordered by his doctor.

Did this person make his neurological Lyme disease worse with vitamin C? Did vitamin C inhibit the success of later treatment with antibiotics? Without a good animal study, it is impossible to know for sure.

Does Vitamin C Worsen Lyme?

What mechanisms are at work? We don't know what role vitamin C might play in the exacerbation of Lyme disease symptoms. What we do know is that, in the laboratory, *Borrelia burgdorferi* prefers to grow and reproduce in a slightly acidic environment. While our body tries to closely regulate blood pH with a buffering mechanism, mega doses of vitamin C can make the pH more acidic, especially in tissues such as joints and the brain.

Some antibiotics, such as macrolides (doxycycline, Biaxin, Zithromax, erythromycin, etc.), are more effective in a slightly alkaline environment. Perhaps vitamin C inhibits the effectiveness of some antibiotics.

A food source for the Lyme spirochete may be one or more of the molecular components that make up human collagen and connective tissue. Specifically, N-acetyl-glucosamine has been determined as a likely food source and the bacteria may possibly even bind to this molecule during infection. Collagen production in the human body is enhanced by the addition of vitamin C. This is why cuts and wounds heal faster in studies on animals when levels of vitamin C are increased. Can vitamin C's effects on collagen production contribute to a more favorable environment for the spirochete? We don't know, but a well designed animal study could probably give us some answers.

Another factor in worsening neurological symptoms may come from the fact that the brain actually expends energy to get higher concentrations of vitamin C across the blood brain barrier. The brain needs higher levels of vitamin C than any other tissue. Can increased levels of vitamin C in the brain enhance the conditions for Lyme infection to thrive?

We don't have any animal or human data to compare, but we do know that vitamin C plays a small but significant role in the production of a neurotoxin called quinolinic acid. Even modest increases in quinolinic acid can cause brain neurons to repeatedly fire. If left unchecked, elevated quinolinic acid levels can lead to demyelination [loss of the myelin sheath around nerve cells] and cell death. This is the main cause of dementia in late-stage AIDS patients. At least one study has suggested that quinolinic acid levels in neurological Lyme patients can be 40x higher than normal. Could these levels go higher if the patient takes mega doses of vitamin C?

In a large patient study that reviewed vitamin supplement use in AIDS patients, it was found that not only did zinc not help improve symptoms, but any amount of zinc actually correlated to a worsening of the disease and a shortening of life. Normally zinc is considered an immune boosting supplement, but zinc supplementation is now contraindicated in AIDS patients. Since we know from this experience that some supplements can exacerbate and worsen symptoms in certain diseases (with dire consequences), then we must use caution in considering treating diseases with mega doses of any supplement.

What may make sense for treating a cold may not make sense for an AIDS patient—or, perhaps, even a Lyme patient.

Studies Are Needed

These are fairly broad speculations, but there is growing anecdotal evidence that vitamin C and perhaps some other mega nutritional therapies are either inhibiting the healing process, increasing symptoms or, even worse, exacerbating the infection. Until a well designed study chooses to look into the role vitamin C and other supplements play in this infection, we will never know the true role that mega nutritional supplements play.

In addition to the three cases I've described, in talking to dozens of other neurological Lyme patients who were taking vitamin C, it seemed—almost without exception—that the higher the dose of vitamin C, the more severe their symptoms were. This is anecdotal evidence only, but considering the tragic outcomes I have seen, I feel that the consumption of unusually high doses of vitamin C by neurological Lyme patients should be reconsidered.

Please remember that not everything natural is good for you. Remember Socrates's last words, "I just drank what?"

---

1. Socrates was an ancient Greek philosopher; he died after being sentenced to drink a cup of poison made from the plant hemlock.

Periodical and Internet Sources Bibliography

The following articles have been selected to supplement the diverse views presented in this chapter.

Berkeley Wellness   "Can Supplements Fight Colds?," n.d. www
                         .berkeleywellness.com.

Martina M. Cartwright   "Zinc and the Common Cold: Just the Facts,"
                         Food for Thought (blog), *Psychology Today*,
                         March 7, 2011. www.psychologytoday.com.

Daily Telegraph   "Health Advice: Insomnia," March 12, 2013.
(London)

R. Morgan Griffin   "Natural Cold and Flu Remedies," WebMD,
                         n.d. www.webmd.com.

Jenny Hope   "Could Zinc Be a Cure for the Common Cold?
                         Taking Supplements Could Shorten Illness
                         Length by 40 Per Cent," *Daily Mail* (London),
                         July 27, 2011.

Ryan Hurd   "The Health Risks of Valerian," Livestrong.com,
                         July 15, 2010. www.livestrong.com.

Timothy   "Valerian: A Safe and Effective Herbal Sleep
Morgenthaler   Aid?," Mayo Clinic, n.d. www.mayoclinic.com.

Office of   "Valerian," n.d. http://ods.od.nih.gov.
Dietary Supplements

For Further Discussion

Chapter 1

1. Which provides better regulation of dietary supplements, the United States or Europe? Explain your answer, citing from the viewpoints in this chapter.

2. If an herb has been used for generations to treat the common cold, do you think that that herb should be forced to pass scientific tests before it is approved for use? Why or why not?

Chapter 2

1. Should you take vitamin supplements just in case they might have a benefit? Why or why not?

2. Based on the evidence in this chapter, do you think calcium supplements are beneficial? Why or why not? Who should take them, if anyone? Why?

Chapter 3

1. Imagine there were an athletic supplement that would improve your performance but that would not show up in drug tests. Would it be fair for athletes to take that supplement? Why or why not?

2. Do you think a weight-loss supplement could actually lead you to gain weight? Might Ben Goldacre's viewpoint about vitamins in chapter 2 also apply to weight loss? Why or why not? Cite information from the viewpoints in this chapter.

Chapter 4

1. Does it seem like it would be dangerous to take supplements to fight the common cold or insomnia? Why or why not? Cite from the viewpoints in your answer.

2. Based on the viewpoints by Wrinn and Grier, would you recommend taking vitamin supplements to aid in the symptoms of Lyme disease? Why or why not?

Organizations to Contact

The editors have compiled the following list of organizations concerned with the issues debated in this book. The descriptions are derived from materials provided by the organizations. All have publications or information available for interested readers. The list was compiled on the date of publication of the present volume; the information provided here may change. Be aware that many organizations take several weeks or longer to respond to inquiries, so allow as much time as possible.

American Herbal Pharmacopoeia (AHP)
PO Box 66809, Scotts Valley, CA   95067
(831) 461-6318; or (831) 438-2196
e-mail: ahp@herbal-ahp.org
website: www.herbal-ahp.org

AHP is a nonprofit organization that promotes the responsible use of herbal products and herbal medicines. It does this by publishing critically reviewed documents called monographs that explain how to ensure the identity, purity, and quality of raw botanical materials. The monographs also include reviews of scientific literature.

Consumer Healthcare Products Association (CHPA)
900 Nineteenth St. NW, Ste. 700, Washington, DC   20006
(202) 429-9260 • fax: (202) 223-6835
e-mail: efunderburk@chpa-info.org
website: www.chpa-info.org

CHPA is a member-based association representing the leading manufacturers and distributors of nonprescription, over-the-counter medicines and dietary supplements. It is committed to promoting the increasingly vital role of over-the-counter medicines and dietary supplements in America's health care system through science, education, and advocacy. The association provides leadership and guidance on regulatory and scientific issues to Congress; state legislatures; and federal, state, and international government agencies. It publishes the quarterly *OTC Connections*, as well as white papers, reports, brochures, and other materials available through its website.

Council for Responsible Nutrition (CRN)
1828 L St. NW, Ste. 510, Washington, DC   20036-5114
(202) 204-7700 • fax: (202) 204-7701
e-mail webmaster@crnusa.org
website: www.crnusa.org

CRN is the leading trade association representing dietary supplement manufacturers and ingredient suppliers. It formulates guidelines for industry ethics and best practices and organizes a national conference. Its website includes information about supplements and industry regulation, as well as press releases.

European Food Safety Authority (EFSA)
Via Carlo Magno 1A, Parma   43126
   ITALY
+39 0521 036111 • fax: +39 0521 036110
e-mail: press@efsa.europa.eu
website: www.efsa.europa.eu

EFSA is the keystone of European Union (EU) risk assessment regarding food and feed safety. In close collaboration with national authorities, EFSA provides independent scientific advice and clear communication on existing and emerging risks. EFSA publishes its scientific outputs and opinions in the *EFSA Journal*. It also publishes supporting publications. Its website includes many articles related to dietary supplements.

International Alliance of Dietary/Food Supplement Associations (IADSA)
50 Rue de l'Association, Brussels   B-1000
   BELGIUM
+32 2 209 11 55 • fax: +32 2 223 30 64

e-mail: secretariat@iadsa.be
website: www.iadsa.org

IADSA is the leading international expert association focused on food supplements. IADSA works to create a sound legislative and political environment for the development of the food supplement sector worldwide. The association's website includes numerous publications on policy, science, and technical issues related to supplements, as well as news updates.

Mayo Clinic
13400 E. Shea Blvd., Scottsdale, AZ   85259
(480) 301-8000
website: www.mayoclinic.org

The Mayo Clinic is a not-for-profit medical practice, medical research group, and medical school with locations in Minnesota (original), Arizona, and Florida. Besides delivering health care, part of its mission includes education and outreach. To fulfill that goal, it has established MayoClinic.com, a website that includes extensive information about numerous health conditions and treatments. The site has many articles on dietary supplements, including "Take Vitamin Supplements with Caution."

The Natural Products Association (NPA)
1773 T St. NW, Washington, DC   20009
(202) 223-0101; toll-free: (800) 966-6632 • fax: (202) 223-0250
e-mail: natural@npainfo.org
website: www.npainfo.org

The NPA is a nonprofit organization dedicated to the natural products industry, including food, dietary supplements, and health & beauty aids. It lobbies at the national level for safe, effective, and accessible natural products. It publishes a number of newsletters, including *NPA Now, NPA Fact of the Week,* and *Natural News Update.* Its website also includes news and articles for consumers, retailers, and suppliers.

NSF International

PO Box 130140, 789 N. Dixboro Rd.
Ann Arbor, MI   48113-0140
(734) 769-8010; toll-free: (800) 673-6275 • fax: (734) 769-0109
e-mail: info@nsf.org
website: www.nsf.org

NSF International is an independent not-for-profit organization that provides standards development, product certification, auditing, education, and risk management for public health and the environment. It publishes standards and reports on numerous health issues, including dietary supplements, which are available for purchase through its website.

US Food and Drug Administration (FDA)

10903 New Hampshire Ave., Silver Spring, MD   20993-0002
toll-free: (888) 463-6332
e-mail: consumer@fda.gov
website: www.fda.gov

The FDA is the agency of the US Department of Health and Human Services responsible for the regulation and supervision of food, drug, and medical appliance safety. Its website includes many reports and articles about dietary supplements and other food and drug issues.

US Pharmacopeial Convention (USP)

12601 Twinbrook Pkwy., Rockville, MD   20852-1790
(301) 881-0666; toll-free: (800) 227-8772
website: www.usp.org

The USP is a nonprofit scientific organization that sets standards for the identity, strength, quality, and purity of medicines, food ingredients, and dietary supplements manufactured, distributed, and consumed worldwide. The USP's drug standards are enforceable in the United States by the Food and Drug Administration, and these standards are developed and relied upon in more than 140 countries. The USP's website includes articles and information on the dietary supplements standards, as well as white papers, newsletters, and other information.

Bibliography of Books

Jennifer Ackerman

Ah-Choo!: The Uncommon Life of Your Common Cold. New York: Hachette, 2010.

Julian Bailes and John McCloskey

When Winning Costs Too Much: Steroids, Supplements, and Scandal in Today's Sports World. Lanham, MD: Taylor Trade, 2005.

Stephen R. Bown

Scurvy: How a Surgeon, a Mariner, and a Gentleman Solved the Greatest Medical Mystery of the Age of Sail. New York: St. Martin's, 2003.

Ralph Campbell and Andrew W. Saul

The Vitamin Cure for Children's Health Problems: Prevent and Treat Children's Health Problems Using Nutrition and Vitamin Supplementation. Laguna Beach, CA: Basic Health, 2012.

Daniel Carpenter

Reputation and Power: Organizational Image and Pharmaceutical Regulation at the FDA. Princeton, NJ: Princeton University Press, 2010.

Brian Clement

Supplements Exposed: The Truth They Don't Want You to Know About Vitamins, Minerals, and Their Effects on You. Franklin Lakes, NJ: Career, 2010.

Chris Cooper

Run, Swim, Throw, Cheat: The Science Behind Drugs in Sport. New York: Oxford University Press, 2012.

| S.J. Enna and
Stata Norton | *Herbal Supplements and the Brain:
Understanding the Benefits and
Hazards.* Upper Saddle River, NJ:
Pearson, 2012. |

| James J. Gormley | *Health at Gunpoint: The FDA's Silent
War Against Health Freedom.* Garden
City Park, NY: SquareOne, 2013. |

| M.R.C.
Greenwood and
Maria Oria, eds. | *Use of Dietary Supplements by
Military Personnel.* Athens, GA:
National Academies Press, 2008. |

| Fran Hawthorne | *Inside the FDA: The Business and
Politics Behind the Drugs We Take
and the Food We Eat.* Hoboken, NJ:
Wiley, 2005. |

| Philip J. Hilts | *Protecting America's Health: The FDA,
Business, and One Hundred Years of
Regulation.* New York: Knopf, 2003. |

| Dan Hurley | *Natural Causes: Death, Lies and
Politics in America's Vitamin and
Herbal Supplement Industry.* New
York: Broadway Books, 2006. |

| Zina Kroner | *Vitamins and Minerals.* Santa
Barbara, CA: Greenwood, 2011. |

| Merrily A. Kuhn
and David
Winston | *Winston & Kuhn's Herbal Therapy
and Supplements: A Scientific and
Traditional Approach.* Philadelphia:
Lippincott, Williams, and Wilkins,
2008. |

| Penny Le Couteur
and Jay Burreson | *Napoleon's Buttons: How 17 Molecules
Changed History.* New York: Penguin,
2003. |

David Lightsey   *Muscles, Speed, and Lies: What the Sport Supplement Industry Does Not Want Athletes or Consumers to Know.* Guilford, CT: Lyons, 2006.

Pamela Mason   *Dietary Supplements.* 4th ed. London: Pharmaceutical Press, 2011.

Michael T. Murray and Joseph Pizzorno   *The Encyclopedia of Natural Medicine.* 3rd ed. New York: Atria, 2012.

Stephanie Silberman and Charles Morin   *The Insomnia Workbook: A Comprehensive Guide to Getting the Sleep You Need.* Oakland, CA: New Harbinger, 2008.

Peter N. Stearns   *Fat History: Bodies and Beauty in the Modern West.* 2nd ed. New York: New York University Press, 2002

Robert Thompson and Kathleen Barnes   *The Calcium Lie: What Your Doctor Doesn't Know Could Kill You.* Brevard, NC: Intruth Press, 2008.

David Tyrrell and Michael Fielder   *Cold Wars: The Fight Against the Common Cold.* New York: Oxford University Press, 2002.

Geoffrey P. Webb   *Dietary Supplements and Functional Foods.* 2nd ed. Hoboken, NJ: Wiley-Blackwell, 2011.

Susan Yager   *The Hundred Year Diet: America's Voracious Appetite for Losing Weight.* New York: Rodale, 2010.

Index

A

Achlorhydria, 87
Adams, John, 36
Adenoma risk, 94
Adequate Intake (AI), 86, 93
Adolescent Invulnerability Scale, 82
AdvoCare, 134, 136–137
Alcohol use, 92, 147
Amenorrhea, 90
American Academy of Pediatrics, 111
American College of Sports Medicine, 138
American Dietetic Association, 73, 79
American Heart Association (AHA), 50, 102
American Herbal Products Association, 35
Amyotrophic Lateral Sclerosis (ALS), 167
Anding, Roberta, 73, 79
Anson, George, 14–15
Antimony exposure, 40–42
Archives of Internal Medicine (journal), 22, 78
Arginine Extreme, 134, 136
Aristolochia herb, 24–25, 54
Aronson, J.K., 56
Aschwanden, Christie, 133–140
ATF Fitness, 40
Athletic supplements
    care in taking, 128–132
    danger from, 133–140

dubious claims of, 139–140
no evidence of effectiveness, 137–138
overview, 129, 131–132, 134
protein and muscles, 129–130
safety problems, 135–136
survey of, *137*
tainting of, 134–135
vitamins and minerals in, 130–131
Australia, 56, 118, 154
Autism spectrum disorder, 41–42
Axiolytic (anxiety inhibitor), 158

B

Balanced diet
    calcium from, 94
    impact of, 70, 129
    micronutrients from, 79
    supplements and, 28, 73
    Vitamin A and, 108
Barefoot, Robert, 143
Barrett, Stephen, 143
Bay Area Laboratory Co-operative (BALCO), 140
Baylor College of Medicine, 22
Beanfreaks, 63
Belgium, 24
Beta carotene. *See* Vitamin A
Beta-glucans, 122
Bioresearch Monitoring program, 49
Biorhythm SSIN Juice, 136
Body-building, 34, 129, 136
Bonds, Barry, 140
Bone health, 92–94

Z